D1432904

All about the
Samoyed

Beryl and Geoff Grounds

22.46

contents

acknowledgements

We are most grateful to the following for readily and generously supplying us with many photographs and items of information:

Ada and Ron Aylward, Wendy and Tom Beaton, Chris Brooks, Serena Brownlie-Sykes, Sheila and David Cox, Audrey Dadds, Angela Danvers-Smith and Terry Smith, Joan Dobson, Wendy and John Drummond, Denise Edmondson, Bridget Enticott, Paul and Jane Farrington, Hazel Fitzgibbon, Carol Fox, Val Freer, Helen Gabb, Gill Genever, Avis Haffenden, Chris and Peter Hale, Pat Hemmings, Gina Hounslow, Birgit Eistrup Jensen, Kirsten Jørgensen, Rose Lewis, Vicky Lloyd, Roly Miller, Betty Moody, Ivor Munday, Granville Pyne, Ken Rawlings, Marie and John Rees, Ian Ross, the Samoyed Association, Elspeth Sayle, Anna Maria Serra, Nick Smit, Jill H Smoot, Sarah Styles, Yvonne Sydenham-Clarke, Zena Thorn Andrews, Carol Walker, Margaret Wilcock, Gina Willis.

Front cover
Ch Annecy's A Winter's Tale.
Photo: David L Lindsay.

foreword

Much of this book assumes you are a newcomer to the world of Samoyeds and also to showing. However, we hope there are also points of interest for those who already possess one of these lovely dogs and would like to know more.

The dog world affords people much pleasure and stimulates a significant amount of business activity and employment as well, so it is no bad thing. What distinguishes it from many activities is the fact that the basic unit, the dog, is an object of love and affection that repays immeasurably the work you put in.

If the show scene is not for you, or you have a puppy that is unlikely to win in any show ring, you have no less potential for delight in having this dog as part of your family or your sole companion. A Samoyed can be a wonderful friend, whether its face fits the Breed Standard or not. One of us had a Samoyed in the family for many years without ever going to a show and the breed's ancestral owners had no thoughts of that kind of competition.

A brief encounter may prompt you to ask why the breed has its particular characteristics, especially why Samoyeds consider themselves so much the friends of all human beings. Where did they come from and what made them like this? Are they as perfect as first impressions may suggest or can there be problems to owning one? When you see a picture of an entrancing little Samoyed puppy, or pick one up and look into its soft, serene eyes as it sits patiently in your arms, it is so easy to decide on the spot that having one must be unadulterated delight. Are there hidden pitfalls?

We hope this book will give you a balanced view of life with Samoyeds. Whether you are the prospective owner of a much-loved pet, a potential breeder and show ring enthusiast, a prospective judge, a participator in one or more of the dog sports applicable to the breed, a historian or just an interested spectator, we hope we can pass to you something of the joy and elation we have experienced over the years in the company of these fascinating and beautiful dogs.

Beryl and Geoff Grounds

CHAPTER
one

Looking Back

To understand Samoyeds thoroughly you need to appreciate their historical background because it is only very recently, in terms of their heredity, that they have lived in homes such as ours. When looking back it's all too easy to take as the breed's starting point the time when people around the world became aware of the dogs through polar exploration. In historical terms that is only an eyeblink away. The story begins so far back that we can only guess at its origins.

Siberia, a really huge part of the world's land surface, has one of the very harshest climates. Nevertheless, as far as recorded history stretches, groups of people have lived there. For obvious reasons these tended to be family units loosely united in tribes. Some of these, like others in Lappland, depended on reindeer for food, clothing and shelter. They developed a pattern of life that remained constant through the ages right up to the present day, though now their way of life, inevitably, is being changed by spreading technology.

The population was always very sparse. A single family might not meet another for a year because the reindeer of near neighbours would compete for the meagre food supply. That fact made annual get-togethers short. So, in complete isolation, a family would take its herd south into the vast forests for the winter and migrate northwards once a year for the short burst of the Siberian summer. The food they searched for was moss, rich in nutrients and adequate in fibre when found in sufficient quantity. It survives well under snow, tolerates being frozen hard, and is capable of amazingly rapid growth when conditions ease. Huge areas of land in the vicinity of the Ob and Jenesei rivers and the Jamal peninsular are marked on maps as marshes, which in summer are a maze of surface water courses and in winter are frozen tundra.

The reindeer herders kept dogs. They must have done so for hundreds, perhaps thousands, of years, for the very earliest recorded visitors reported the fact. Because so many of the world's breeds have histories based upon utilitarian value it is easy to surmise that this was the case with Samoyeds. You look at what most will do instinctively, which is to pull you with great strength whenever you put leads on them, and conclude they were developed by man from their genetic ancestors, wolves, to pull sledges because there's so much snow in Siberia.

This is dubious. If you lived there and twice a year had to pack up your entire possessions for a trek of many hundreds of miles, carrying your hefty reindeer skin tents and poles, your cooking pots and clothes, your bedding and children, tools and furniture, would you really put it all on a sledge pulled by dogs when you had a herd of reindeer travelling with you? We're not at all surprised to find that herders in Siberia today are to be seen travelling with very substantial sledges pulled by their reindeer.

Sources of Samoyed characteristics

Reports from early travellers mention the dogs pulling boats, and this is much more credible as the source of Samoyed pulling instincts. The mass of water courses brought into existence by the surprisingly warm Siberian summer would offer convenient and possibly rapid travel using a lighter means of power. The dogs would have an advantage over the reindeer scrambling along marshy banks, and a boat needs much less dragging than a heavily-laden sledge on snow across uneven ground.

A Nenet family voting on 10 June 1996 in the Russian Presidential Election in the Jamal Peninsular. The dog in the foreground looks very similar to the original Samoyed imports.
Photo: Associated Press

The Samoyed

The dogs have another instinct not so readily seen in Britain because other breeds do this work more precisely: herding. We are convinced this was their main working use. Imagine the scene: whether on the move or grazing in one place a herd of reindeer roam over a sizable area. Keeping them organised to an extent and not letting them roam so far they cannot be retrieved would be quite a problem for the few members of a family whose only transport was a reindeer-drawn sledge. How much more convenient to breed dogs capable of running with endurance rather than speed, intelligent and independent, with an instinct for keeping the animals reasonably together, and possessing a powerful and excited bark to let people know where they were and to warn whenever something unusual was at hand.

We've seen an excellent example of the herding trait in Samoyeds. We took a five-year-old bitch on holiday and were walking along a track in Devon when she heard sheep. We can say positively she had never seen one in her life until then because we lived in a completely arable farming area. Before we could stop her she leapt up the high bordering bank, found a gap in the thick hedge and disappeared from sight. Quite distraught at the thought of what might happen, we ran with our sons to find a gate. In the field there was at first no sign, nor sound, of sheep or the bitch, but we could see the land sloping away from us. Where on earth had she gone, we wondered anxiously?

Then a flock of some 50 sheep breasted the rise, running at reasonable speed, nicely grouped and in no way bothered. The bitch was running to and fro close behind, pushing first her left side along the flanks of nearby sheep, then her right as she quartered. The flock moved in a wide arc and then disappeared out of sight again. We raced after her and looked down the long slope of the field to see her swing them around at the bottom and bring them back towards us again. As she neared us we shouted yet again for her to come away, fearful of the actions of the farmer if he also was watching. The bitch, now panting heavily, gave us a despairing look as if to say, 'Will you please tell me where to take this lot?' Finally she got the message that we didn't want them at all, broke away and came back to us. The sheep immediately began grazing again, quite unflurried. The bitch, whose actions had been pure instinct, couldn't understand why we were not at all pleased.

We can well imagine her ancestors, and maybe her cousins today, roaming freely around the edge of reindeer herds across the almost limitless plains of the tundra, content in their independence, instinctively chivvying the stragglers and moving them gradually onwards on the migration trails.

There is a third key aspect to the instinctive nature of Samoyeds: their great friendliness towards all people. Again, use your imagination about the relationship between the reindeer herders and their dogs. In the exceptionally cruel climate, and with such limited daylight in winter, would you keep your dogs outside? These people may have lived lives we categorise as primitive, but that doesn't mean they were any the less sensitive to feelings of friendship. It's perfectly understandable that they kept the dogs in their homes, loving them, just as we do.

As we were preparing this book we saw the picture on page 7 showing Nenets in the Jamal voting in the 1996 Russian Presidential election. You can see a typical Samoyed right at the front. Either the people and the photographer thought the dog sufficiently noteworthy to be so conspicuous, or the dog thought so and the people were happy to let it take pride of place. Either way, we are looking at dog-lovers.

To summarise: the extended history of the breed tells of a close relationship with small groups of people whose lives were comparatively uncomplex but who needed very great strength and resilience to live in a most uncompromising climate. The dogs were used in various ways, as occasion demanded, but also were loved and loving companions. Because of the dangers of any accident, such as a dog bite, any puppy showing real signs of an unsound temperament would be killed: hence the central characteristic of affection for all humans. That's how they were bred and socialised from way back, however far that may be.

'By any other name...'

Why *Samoyeds*? Where did the name come from? The word carries the meaning of self-sufficiency in the sense of nomadic. It doesn't convey an identity for a particular group of people, but was written across the Siberian maps during the 19th century. The tribes had varied ethnic names, such as Urak, Dolghan, Ostiak, Tungu, Urgu and others. There never was a specific one called *Samoyed* – most were Samoyed, and writers at the beginning of the 20th century referred to groups as the *Ostiak Samoyed*, the *Tungu Samoyed* and so on.

We can imagine something of a comparison in one application we give the word *traveller* today. Travellers seen in their caravans and mobile homes encompass a mixture of people who are self-sufficient. Russians tended to use the word *Samoyed* disparagingly, so the people who were tabbed with the label wanted it removed. Since the 1920s they have been known collectively as *Nenets*. It's interesting that a despised word should now designate such beautiful dogs.

Often the name is mispronounced. You probably know the word *samovar*: three distinct syllables with the *o* pronounced much as most English speakers would say the vowel in the word *hot*. Sam – o – yed is much the same, with *yed* as the third and separate syllable. Of course, with English pronunciation, it is very easy to slur the second and third syllables into Sam – oi – yed, or even Sam – oid. It also gets said as Sammy – yed. Small wonder people abbreviate it to Sam! Incidentally, it was spelt *Samoyede* when first used in the west to refer to the dogs.

The breed is so named as a result of the second and quite short phase of its history, when the dogs came to the notice of westerners. With global business expansion came increased knowledge of breeds around the world, giving impetus to the developing hobby of dog showing. From Britain an electrical engineer, Ernest Kilburn Scott, travelled to the Russian port or Archangel in 1889. Whilst watching timber being unloaded he saw, and bought, a brown puppy with white flashes on its tail, chest and feet. He brought it home for his wife – there were no quarantine restrictions in Britain in those days. It grew into a typical spitz type and was exhibited by the Kilburn Scotts in the foreign dog classes at shows in the 1890s. They named it Sabarka, no doubt from one of the Russian words for dog, *sobaka*. Because it came from what he was told was Samoyed territory, that name was used to classify the breed.

The varied sources of early imports

Nearly four years later, Ernest Kilburn Scott bought a white dog of similar type from a member of the crew of a timber freighter returning from Russia. This one they named Whitey Petchora, the second word being the name of a river (Pecora) flowing from the western slopes of the Ural mountains to the Barents Sea. She also was typically spitz. They mated her to Sabarka and the litter contained white, brown and black puppies, some of whom later appeared in the show ring.

Referring to the origins of the dogs, Ernest Kilburn Scott wrote in his contribution to *The 20th Century Dog*, by Herbert Compton, 1904:

The Samoyede has come to be very domesticated... The Samoyede people are an intelligent race, who have always been within touch of European influence. They are a quiet, inoffensive, pastoral, nomadic people, very fond of their dogs, on whose intelligence they are largely dependent. For example, the Samoyedes will not part with a thoroughly trained dog for any sum of money, as it is practically indispensable to them for herding their herds of reindeer. The dogs live in their masters' houses, and are as well cared for as a shepherd's or a farmer's dog in this country.

The unique intelligence of the Samoyede... is traceable to the number of uses to which it is put, and its close and intimate touch with its human masters. I should feel inclined to liken its position to that of a collie or sheep-dog, for by no other process of argument can you account for its really affectionate and trustworthy disposition.

By 1898 our Kennel Club was celebrating its silver jubilee, so you can understand that during the last quarter of the 19th century dog showing in Britain became thoroughly popular.

The Prince and Princess of Wales on their Silver Wedding in 1888.

From 1873 The Kennel Club's President was the Prince of Wales, later to become King Edward VII. His niece, who married Czar Nicholas II of Russia, sent at least one white dog of Samoyed type to him, and he certainly acquired others of mixed colouring, because a number appeared at shows under his name between 1890 and 1900, examples being Jaego, Perla, Bosco, and Luska. He and his wife, Princess Alexandra of Denmark, were painted with a white dog of Samoyed type in 1888 on the occasion of their silver wedding. These dogs, owned by the royal couple, were naturally the subject of much admiration and it was not long before others tried to obtain similar dogs.

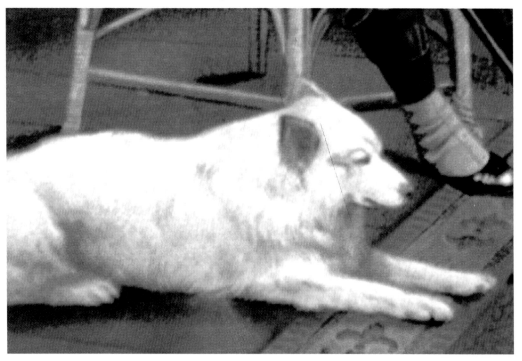

Detail from the picture opposite.
The dog has distinct similarities to the one with the Nenet family on page 7.

In addition to this, over a period of no more than 25 years, global activity brought these and similar dogs much into the public eye. This was the age of polar exploration, the great first treks of humans to the uttermost ends of the earth. Allied to this was the fact that communication was much improved; photographs were taken, reports were serialised in newspapers and magazines and books were published. Most explorers wanted dogs to pull their sledges.

Their first choice was Greenland dogs, for their size, strength and pulling power. When the Danish government restricted the sale of these, agents collected dogs in northern Russia. The various tribes of people they tried to buy from offered a limited and varied mixture. For example, when Alexander Trontheim was commissioned to collect dogs for the Norwegian explorer Fridtjof Nansen in 1893, he acquired only 34 instead of the 40 requested, all males instead of both sexes to increase the stock, and all but four castrated! They were various sizes and colours, but some were more-or-less white. He had one bitch from a previous expedition, a tough and fairly large Newfoundland/Eskimo Dog cross called Kvik who, fortunately for the polar attempt, produced plenty of puppies on two successive seasons – so many that they killed some to leave her with eight each time.

The dogs Captain Jackson brought back to England.
Courtesy: Ken Rawlings

In 1895 Nansen reached the farthest point north so far attained, travelling by sledge with one companion. When unable to progress further they turned back towards the edge of the ice, gradually killing and eating all their dogs, including poor old Kvik. They then paddled back to Norway in collapsible canoes they had taken with them. Since they had previously had their ship, the Fram, steered into the pack ice and allowed it to become frozen in, hoping it would be carried nearer to the Pole, they now had to wait for the ice to melt. Its captain then sailed it back to Norway with some dogs which, as young puppies, had escaped being chosen for the one-way slog with Nansen. They produced descendants but these, it seems, died out later. The captain, Otto Sverdrup, reported in his journal that some of the puppies born to one of them, Suffi, were 'pure white and big and clean. They look like what the Samoyed people call Bjelkiers'. This word is said to refer to white animals that produce white offspring.

In Britain an expedition was put together to make a shot at the Pole. This was sponsored by Alfred Harmsworth, the newspaper proprietor later to become Lord Northcliffe, who no doubt hoped to gain newsworthy items for his paper. The expedition was led by Captain F G Jackson and had as its primary objective a survey of Franz Josef Land. It was thought this might be the southern tip of a northern arctic continent 'balancing' Antarctica. It seems surprising that only 100 years ago we didn't know whether the North Pole was land or sea.

Like Nansen, Jackson collected dogs from northern Russia and his, also, were quite a mixture. Fortunately for us he viewed them rather differently. He recorded various facts about them, particularly that some of the smaller ones were white, weighed 20–27kg (45–60lb), produced similar puppies, were great friends with their human companions, were useless when chastised, and were quite content in the harshest weather. Incredibly, he and his companions spent three years surveying the islands, as he proved them to be. Although he made an attempt to cross the ice northwards towards the Pole, it couldn't have been more than a token sally. The expedition was not adequately supplied and the going across the pack ice was an unending series of ridges over which they had to haul sledges by hand.

On his return in 1897 Jackson brought all his surviving canine companions with him and these were acquired by various interested people, including Princess Alexandra, who received Jacko, and Mr and Mrs Kilburn Scott. Probably the full list was four dogs: Jacko, Nimrod, Russ and Yugor, and four bitches: Flo, Gladys, Jenny and Kvik. Some of these produced offspring who appeared in the show ring and can be seen in the pedigrees of the two early champions Sea Mist and Eastre (see chapter 8, pages 110–111).

As the breed became better known more people tried to import or acquire examples. Lady Sitwell imported Musti and used him at stud. Houdin came from the Italian Duke of Abruzzi's expedition. Mr Colman, who owned a very extensive horse stud farm, bought the bitch Ayesha, imported by Mr Gray Landsberg, and later sold her to Mrs Cammack. She produced offspring who figure in the early pedigrees. Miss Puxley obtained Sam from Russia, mated him to Keena, bought from the Kilburn Scotts, and produced Ch Siberian Keeno.

The breed also attracted the attention of the Hon Mrs McLaren Morrison, a lady who must have been quite a character. She collected a very wide-ranging selection of dogs, cats and other animals and campaigned many of these at shows. She pressed The Kennel Club for some years to give full recognition to the breed and tried to get it far more widely

Ayesha,
acquired by Mr Colman in 1910

known by the public, or rather the readers of the quality magazines, by getting articles featuring Samoyeds printed. The result is quite a rich source of material and photographs for present-day archivists.

One of Mrs McLaren's dogs, Peter The Great, was black. It is interesting to note that by no means all the early Samoyeds that came into Britain were white or nearly so. In the results of shows at which they were exhibited the colour is given in most cases, so we know that the

Prince of Wales' Perla (bitch) was white, Bosco (dog) was sable and white, Sabarka (dog) brown and white as mentioned above, Kathinka, a bitch out of Musti and Whitey Petchora (both white), was black, Pedro, a son of Peter, was black and Peterkin, another of Peter's sons, was brown. However, despite Mrs McLaren Morrison's and other people's partial support for blacks, white or cream must have been dominant, for quite soon black disappeared and even those who tried to breed for it were unsuccessful.

Two southern expeditions used a proportion of Samoyeds, a few of which had an influence on breed development. The first was led by Carsten Borchgrevink, who tried for the South Pole between 1898 and 1900 with dogs from Greenland and Siberia. On his return he off-loaded his dogs south of New Zealand and they were kept on Stewart Island by Arthur Traill, who lived there in some isolation with his family. There were 90, and feeding them became impossible. It was hoped that other expeditions would call in and use them again but no one did so for seven years, by which time most had been killed or given away because of the food shortage. Those spared were all white and certainly Samoyeds. His son, Roy Traill MBE, recorded the facts in 1982 when he was in his late 80s in an article in a New Zealand newspaper.

Sir Ernest Shackleton collected the nine Samoyeds then available on Stewart Island for his first expedition in 1907. There were four dogs and five bitches, which soon gave him a useful supply of puppies. He gave quite detailed accounts of these, with photographs, in his book *First On The Antarctic Continent* (1909). When he returned from that expedition he gave away the remaining dogs to people in New Zealand and Australia, so adding to the number who found their way there.

Captain R F Scott was involved with two expeditions. The first in 1902 took dogs from Siberia, though photographs suggest these were not the same type as Shackleton collected in 1907. For his fateful last expedition he was given three Samoyeds by Mr and Mrs Kilburn Scott (no relation to him), but he didn't think much of them. He dismissed them as 'pretty exotics...

quite unfitted for such arduous work as lay ahead', which suggests he didn't really know the breed or its true origins. One was lost overboard on the journey from Britain and the other two, named Nova after his ship and Lady Scott after his wife, were given away to friends in New Zealand.

The dog lost from the ship was a son of a well-known sire, Antarctic Buck. This dog, famed in breed history, was found by the Kilburn Scotts in Sydney Zoo. Ernest Kilburn Scott had taken a short-term appointment at Sydney University in 1904 and his family joined him later.

Young Samoyeds by Peter the Great, a black owned by The Hon Mrs McLaren Morrison.

Antarctic Buck on board ship.

Buck was an excellent example and the Kilburn Scotts pressed their case to buy him and finally were successful. He came back to Britain with them and was used at stud. When mated to Kviklene and Olgalene he produced future champions (Fang and Kaifas), and his offspring became an important influence in pedigrees. He was born on Borchgrevink's expedition and was given away to people in Hobart as they journeyed south. Mr Kilburn Scott reported Buck's age as 10 on his death in 1909.

Both Sydney and Wellington Zoos had sections exhibiting Samoyed dogs for many years. People in both countries acquired them from varied sources and sometimes took the opportunity of visiting expeditions to use stud dogs on their bitches. Early pedigrees in New Zealand give sires as a *dog on Capt Scott's ship* or a *dog on the Nimrod* (Shackleton's ship).

Others came later to Britain from Russia as various people imported, but few became significant, with the exception of Ayesha. The rather mixed examples that reached here towards the end of the 19th century and the beginning of the 20th therefore served as the foundation stock.There is no doubt that the real driving force behind the development of the breed from what was available was Mrs Kilburn Scott. She didn't seek the limelight – others did that, especially those who liked to appear in the fashionable circle in the show ring. But she, with her husband and later on her own, carried on a breeding programme that thoroughly established the breed we have inherited.

(Top) Farningham dogs in the mid-1920s.

(Above) **Miss Ivy Kilburn Scott in 1927,**
featured in the *Dog World Annual*.

Farningham Samoyeds

After the first world war the Kilburn Scotts, having moved to Kent, took the kennel name *Farningham*. Many notable Samoyeds carried this affix here and abroad, as Farningham stock was much sought after for use in establishing and developing kennels. The influence of Antarctic Buck in their lines was outstanding; so much so that later on another breeder felt it an advertising point to offer puppies without Buck in their pedigrees! The usual breeding pattern was variation on the line breeding theme, and the fact that a recognisable breed emerged quite soon from the starting mixture points to the underlying genetic homogeneity.

We once saw an early picture of dogs taken at the Kilburn Scott kennels. It certainly showed a considerable mixture of type and size, as you might imagine. When they drew up the first breed standard, probably in 1908, they wrote into it points they liked and felt were important from eight different types they could discern. This first standard was an ideal for breeders to aim at rather than a description of an actual dog. The picture of six dogs at Farningham reproduced from an advertisement in a *Dog World Annual* shows their success in developing type.

Of the 14 champions owned or bred by the Kilburn Scotts only two carry the Farningham affix: Ch Polar Light of Farningham, born in 1923, bred by Miss Simon, and Ch Bareena of Farningham, born in 1925. However, the name appears on very many dogs in other champion pedigrees in Britain and abroad, showing that Mrs Kilburn Scott concentrated on breeding rather than showing, especially after the early years. She also judged eminently up to and including 1944, the year she died.

Early breed clubs

Mr Kilburn Scott had much to do with setting up the first breed organisation in 1909, The Samoyede Club. However, it created a rule debarring ladies from standing for its committee. As a result The Ladies' Samoyed Association (they dropped the e) came into existence in 1912 with Mrs Kilburn Scott as its first President. Whether this would have caused a major rift is not known, because the first world war soon erupted, severely curtailing both showing and breeding. The Kennel Club would not allow the registration of dogs, and feeding became so great a problem that at one point the possible introduction of a law restricting each household to one dog only was considered.

After the war male attitudes to women's abilities had undergone welcome change and the two clubs amalgamated at Crufts in 1920 to form the Samoyed Association. The President was Major F G Jackson, and the Vice-Presidents were Mrs Kilburn Scott, The Hon Mrs McLaren Morrison and Mr W Hally.

Ch Olaf Oussa,
the first Samoyed champion.

Breed development

On the whole, those attracted to the breed in the early years of the 20th century were well-to-do. No doubt this was due in part to its rarity and eye-catching appearance, but the fact that Queen Alexandra owned and showed the well-known Jacko also had its effect. She presented a challenge cup which, no doubt, gave an added dimension to ring competition. Separate classification for Samoyeds at shows first occurred in 1902 and The Kennel Club recognised the breed in 1905. Publicity was increasing to the extent that, by the end of the first decade, the breed was firmly established, ownership was spreading, some five or six champions had been made up and some notable future ones born.

Had the first world war not broken out, who knows what major kennels might have emerged in the wake of the Kilburn Scotts'. Looking back over the century we see that the next major kennel did not begin to develop until some 10 years after the war. But that period certainly saw very determined efforts by some very committed people to build up the breed again. One who had a notable effect was Miss J V Thomson-Glover.

Miss Thomson-Glover's account of visiting the Kilburn Scotts' house in Kent to purchase a seven-week-old puppy in 1911 began a short chapter about Snow Cloud, her foundation dog, in the 1961 edition of *The Samoyed*. Fifty-one years later we visited Mrs Dorothy L Perry's Kobe kennels, also in Kent, for the same purpose. That Kobe worthily took on the mantle of Farningham is because Miss Thomson-Glover became a great expert on the breed and advised Mrs Perry for many years. Miss Thomson-Glover herself never adopted a kennel name.

Miss Thomson-Glover gave a lively sketch of the LKA Show at the Botanical Gardens where Snow Cloud not only competed at nine months of age but also beat Mrs Cammack's Ch Kaifas, *as predicted by that lady, who was full of great kindness to such complete novices.* The event, understandably, provided a lifelong memory, focused by *the trees, lawns and flowers, complemented by the long flowing dresses and picture hats of the women... the morning coats and top hats of the men*, in the presence of Queen Alexandra before whom the winners were later paraded. Snow Cloud *received an especial pat.*

Miss Thomson-Glover owned or bred six English champions and one United States champion. Her first was Ch Nada, born in 1915, the result of mating Snow Cloud to Mrs Cammack's imported Ayesha. Another son of Snow Cloud, Silver Cloud (out of Nastja, a granddaughter of Jacko), mated to Ch Nada, produced Ch Eastre, a bitch whose head study (see page 109) remains for many people one of the most outstanding examples of the early years. The last she bred was Ch Edelweiss, born in 1927. Because Snow Cloud came from the Kilburn Scott's kennels he was line-bred to Nansen, born from a mating between two unrelated imports, Musti and Whitey Petchora. Surviving photographs suggest he had many points we would applaud today.

Kobe Samoyeds

In 1928 Mrs Dorothy L Perry bred a litter of 10 Samoyeds, all registered under her kennel name Kobe. She had purchased their dam, Chia of Kobe, and sire, Beardmore Glacier, as puppies from the Kilburn Scotts. Though Kobe seems a most unlikely name it attained worldwide renown in Samoyed affairs for 60 years or so. Mrs Perry first showed and bred Pekingese. She admitted that, when she adopted the kennel name, she thought Kobe was in China. When she had her first Samoyeds the Pekes objected strongly, so they were phased out. Incidentally she was also one of the first people in the country to have Bernese Mountain Dogs, but these also gave place to the Samoyeds.

For many years she lived at Whyteleafe, where *Kobe, Whyteleafe, Surrey* was quite sufficient an address for enquiries from anywhere in the world. She and Miss Thomas-Glover struck up a friendship which was very much to Kobe's advantage. Her first champion was

Kosca of Kobe, bred in 1928 by Mrs Edwards, who lives on in the breed's history particularly because she bred Ch Kara Sea. What we find fascinating is that a litter brother and sister of Kosca were also future champions – Riga of the Arctic and Surf of the Arctic, bought by Miss Keyte-Perry, who was no relation and was to become a distinct rival in the breed.

Manufacturers produced many postcards featuring Samoyeds. This one was posted in Nottingham on 10 April 1933. Courtesy: Margaret Wilcock

Kobe flourished in the years before the second world war and rapidly regained its status afterwards. Mrs Perry's daughter, Mrs Irene Ashfield, gradually took over its management from the late 1950s onwards. By 1982, when she died, 44 champions had borne the famous affix, of which 23 were home-bred. Goodness knows how many others were made up abroad or born directly out of Kobe parents. The affix is now owned by Rene's daughter, Terry.

The kennel developed a most recognisable type, so much so that many people in the breed still refer today to the 'good Kobe type'. It is so difficult to describe in words, but a head with nicely-shaped eyes and a delightful smile immediately comes to mind. The body was firm with good angulation, build was medium and correct in size for the breed standard. Coat was beautifully harsh and movement firm and positive. Of course, they produced 'also-rans', as do all breeders. It is impossible to do otherwise, given the mixture from which the breed started here. But thoughtful line-breeding generally gave excellent results and very many people in Britain and across the world founded kennels from Kobe stock. We were no exception and, when Beryl decided to line-breed to one particular Kobe litter, we developed a type we liked that people soon referred to as the 'Whitewisp type'.

Arctic Samoyeds

For a short while Dorothy Perry and Marion Keyte-Perry

Miss Marion Keyte-Perry with some of her Arctic dogs. Courtesy: Margaret Wilcock

were together on the committee of the Samoyed Association, as was Miss Thomson-Glover. A rift developed in the early 1930s over the question of whether coat colour should be white without exception (the protagonist for 'all white' being *KP*), or whether cream and biscuit shading was needed to preserve true quality (as insisted by *TG*). The result was the founding of the British Samoyed Club, which for many years was synonymous with Marion Keyte-Perry. No doubt very different human temperaments also played a part in the schism, for *KP* was delightfully eccentric in her vision of her position in society as well as in breed affairs. She was Principal of Oak Hall, a girls' private school, and later Chairman of the Ladies' Branch of The Kennel Club. She wrote a book on the breed in 1962 in which she refers to the setting up of the British Samoyed Club:

I was then intensely interested in my Samoyed activities and it seemed to me that a much wider sphere could be reached if social gatherings could be achieved to bring the personnel together in addition to the contacts made in the competitive show ring.

Her Arctic kennel depended more on the purchase of stock from other kennels than did Kobe, probably because of her determination to have only pure white coats. As a result her breeding was more mixed. She mentions in her book, under 'Breeding', that 'hundreds of puppies have been bred in my Arctic Kennels'. Much of the work was undertaken by kennel maids, no doubt assisted by school girls. Seventeen champions bore her affix, the last four being bitches: two litter sisters born in 1944, Ch Dawn of the Arctic and Ch Wings of the Arctic, and two others born in 1945, Ch Honor of the Arctic and Ch Aura of the Arctic. There is no doubt from photographs of groups of Arctic stock that she developed a recognisable type but, as far as heads and expressions are concerned, we feel Kobe had a distinct edge.

Snowland Samoyeds

Mrs Ada Westcott's Snowland kennel in the West Country also bridged the war by many years. She bred far more than she showed, so success for her stock in the ring usually came from other owners of Snowland dogs. She also exported considerably, particularly to Scandinavia, Canada and the United States of America. Eight English champions bore her kennel name. Again, a particular type comes to mind, especially notable for dense and harsh coat quality.

The breed abroad

In the early years the Kilburn Scotts exported Samoyeds to a number of other countries, as did other people who developed early breeding lines. English-bred stock, therefore, appears far back in pedigrees in Australasia, Europe, North America and South Africa. A limited number of Samoyeds reached those countries by other routes.

Limitations on the size of this book preclude a survey of the breed in other countries. However, the Kalina Kennel in Australia, developed by Yvonne Sydenham-Clarke, certainly deserves mention alongside the three highlighted above. Born and brought up in England, Yvonne married and went to Australia in 1951 where she imported foundation champion stock from Kobe. From then and up to the present the kennel has achieved exceptionally out-

Int Ch Imperial Rebel of Kobe, imported into Australia by Yvonne Sydenham-Clarke, pictured with his granddaughter, Ch Kalina Imperial Eleban.

standing success in the show ring, including the pinnacle of Best in Show awards at the Sydney Royal. She has continued to import top-quality dogs from Great Britain and elsewhere from time to time and, in her turn, has exported to many other countries for others to found kennels, particularly to New Zealand.

To the present day

The effects of the austerity period forced upon us following the second world war lasted for nearly 10 years, after which dog ownership expanded once again. Interest in the breed became much more widespread and registrations gradually increased. In more recent years the figures were as follows:

1986	1987	1988	1989	1990	1991	1992	1993	1994	1995	1996
732	851	769	1301	1335	1286	1170	1181	1270	1247	1212

You can see that, after the sharp increase in 1989, numbers levelled again; the average for the eight years 1989–1996 was 1250, with the annual deviation quite small. Assuming an average life of 12 years for British Samoyeds, the above figures suggest there are about 13,500 living registered Samoyeds in the country. The marked rise in registrations is due in part to an increase in the number of puppies being bred in puppy farms alongside many other breeds. The breed has increased in popularity and more people show than was the case, say, 30 years ago. However, entries at shows have declined somewhat because of the rise in entry fees. Most exhibits now are entered in only one, or perhaps two, classes per show.

Naturally, the post-war expansion went hand-in-glove with the establishment of many more kennels from the 1950s onwards. Inevitably, to mention some and not others does a disservice to a number of devoted supporters of the breed. Some which we feel have developed particular types and/or achieved a creditable number of champions over a significant period are:

Annecy:	Margaret (and formerly Vinny) Wilcock, and Robin Newhouse
Crownie:	Muriel Hopkin and her son John, (now) Judge Hopkin
Crensa:	John and Betty James
Delmonte:	Robin Lings
Fairvilla:	Eileen (and formerly Tiny) Danvers, now Eileen and her daughter, Angela Danvers-Smith
Golway:	Betty Poole
Novaskaya:	Betty Moody
Samont:	Thelma and Derek Pont
Samovar:	Ivor Munday
Snowcryst:	Rose Lewis
Snowmyth:	Leslie Morgan
Sworddale:	formerly Bunty Ross, now Olive Hampton
Whitewisp:	Our own
Zamoyski:	Carol and Jim Hamilton

Many people have founded kennels based on the lines these kennels have developed, and they based theirs on others further back. The process continues. Other breeders whose stock shines in the show ring today may well figure in future publications as other writers identify key kennels. Development of a distinctive and correct type within the breed standard is an elusive but fascinating pursuit demanding considerable commitment of thought, time, effort and considerable expense. Travelling and showing, feeding, kennels and runs, health checks and treatment are all costly these days. Many people who thoroughly enjoy showing do not have the resources to keep the fairly large number of dogs necessary to produce a specific type.

However, for all involved with the breed in any way, being part of the on-going history of the relationship these dogs have had with humans over perhaps thousands of years is surely a jewel to be treasured. They, like us, make their genetic contribution to the scheme of things which, perhaps, is too large for us to see in overview.

A personal glance

In 1927 a litter of Samoyeds was whelped by Mrs R M Hilliard, whose affix was Asgard. She bestowed on them proud Nordic names, one of which was Hakon of Asgard. In *The Kennel Gazette* of April 1928 there is an entry recording his transfer. In the November 1928 issue there is an entry recording a second transfer.

In 1931 Beryl's father, walking between the station and his office in Cardiff, regularly saw a Samoyed tied on a short lead and restricted to a very small yard. Though he knew hardly anything about the breed, annoyance at the dog's lonely existence got the better of him. He sought out and informed the owner that he was buying the dog. He took possession there and then, returned home as usual to Newport and presented the dog to the family, particularly to Beryl, then aged two.

So Hakon of Asgard entered his fourth and final home to begin a far happier life. He had in full measure the breed's characteristics of intelligence, love of people, and independence. Perhaps due to his early restricted life 'Harky' took any slight chance to slip out of the house and explore the neighbourhood. Not content with walking, he indulged the breed's love of rides on moving vehicles. He would board trams, travel to the terminus and return, knowing instinctively which was 'his' stop to get off and amble home. Obviously eye-catching, he became well known to the tram conductors, who were intrigued by his skill and tolerated his occasional stolen pleasure.

In memory he was truly wonderful. Photographs don't do him justice by a 1000%. The few remaining suggest he wouldn't figure highly in today's show winners' statistics; more probably not at all. But in Beryl's view he was an inestimable champion.

That affection is the reward for owning a Samoyed – the gift bestowed on us across the centuries by loving, nomadic folk who have touched the greater spirit of life and offered us this enthralling manifestation.

Hakon of Asgard with a very young Beryl Grounds and her brother.

CHAPTER
two

A Survey of
Breed Standards

A breed standard is a formal statement of a specific breed's characteristics with details of the various bodily parts and attributes, such as gait and disposition. When a new breed is first recognised by The Kennel Club, people interested in it, owners, breeders and, probably, importers are consulted, usually through the agency of a breed club if one exists. If the breed exists in another country where a controlling organisation publishes a breed standard, that serves as a useful basis. However, in the early days of Samoyed imports no such base existed. The Samoyed Breed Standard was first drawn up by members of The Samoyede Club, founded in 1909, acting under the leadership of Ernest Kilburn Scott, and it was adopted by The Kennel Club.

In time it may be considered necessary to change the wording of a standard. In some breeds this is because breeders have deliberately emphasised certain points to the extent that the dogs' appearance has significantly changed. In others, breed clubs may feel that wording is insufficiently clear, or is being misinterpreted. When this happens application is made to The Kennel Club to consider changes. In some cases The Kennel Club may decide for its own reasons to change the wording. It can do so without consultation, because it owns the copyright. In practice it consults closely with breed clubs, but then makes the final decision.

Breed standards may vary between countries, probably not a great deal but nevertheless in significant detail. It is important to know these differences if, for example, you are to judge abroad, when you must use the standard of the country in which you are judging. Another reason might be if you are selecting a puppy to go overseas. If you know that a greater height is allowable it would not be sensible to send a puppy from stock that you know is on the small side. The Fédération Cynologique Internationale (FCI) and the American Kennel Club Standards (AKC) both allow slightly larger Samoyeds than do The Kennel Club Breed Standard and other national standards based on this.

We give here the original standard, the 1967 full revision and the 1987 revision for which The Kennel Club adopted an identical format for all standards. We have also included the standards used on the continent (FCI) and in America (AKC). This should give you a picture of the changes that have occurred over time and between countries.

HISTORICAL BREED STANDARDS

Fortunately, many people have tried to keep Samoyeds as close to the originals as possible and have, thank goodness, not wanted to introduce 'cosmetic' changes as has been the case with some other breeds. We hope everyone connected with the breed wants to keep to that ideal. Nevertheless the dogs have changed, as a result of different feeding, living less active lives in very different climates, invariably having mates decided for them rather than the 'natural' pack order, having regular veterinary treatment, and so forth. We think you can see that the standards have taken these 'nurture' changes into account.

Samoyeds at a Scottish show in the 1930s. Eleven carry the Viking affix.

The Original Samoyed Breed Standard

General Appearance: The Samoyed, being essentially a working dog, should be strong and active and graceful, and as his work lies in cold climates his coat should be heavy and weather-resisting. He should not be long in back, as a weak back would make him practically useless for his legitimate work; but at the same time a cobby body, such as the Chow's, would also place him at a great disadvantage as a draught dog. Breeders should aim for the happy medium - viz, a body not long, but muscular, allowing liberty, with a deep chest and well-sprung ribs, and exceptionally strong loin. A full grown dog should stand about 21in at the shoulder. On account of the depth of chest required, the legs should be moderately long; a very short-legged dog is to be deprecated. Hindquarters should be particularly well developed, stifles well bent, and any suggestions of unsound stifles or cow hocks severely penalised.

Coat: The body should be well covered with thick, close, soft, and short undercoat, with harsh hair growing through it, forming the outer coat, which should stand straight away from the body.

Head: A broad, flat skull, muzzle of medium length, a tapering foreface, not too sharply defined, ears not too long and slightly rounded at tips, set well apart, and well covered inside with long hair. Eyes dark, large and full, with alert intelligent expression. Lips black. Hair short and smooth before the ears. Nose and eye-rims black for preference, but may be brown or flesh-coloured. Mouth level, with large and strong teeth.

Back: Medium in length, broad and very muscular.

Chest and Ribs: Chest broad and deep. Ribs well sprung, giving plenty of heart and lung room.

Hindquarters: Very muscular, stifles well let down, cow-hocks or straight stifles very objectionable.

Legs: Stout, straight and muscular.
Feet: Flattish and well spread, thickly padded.
Tail: Heavy, and carried well over the back.
Weight: Dogs up to 50lb; bitches up to 40lb.
Colour: All colours permissible; white preferred.

Scale of points	Value
General appearance	10
Coat	15
Head	15
Size	10
Chest and ribs	10
Hindquarters	10
Back	10
Feet	8
Legs	7
Tail	5
Total	**100**

An excellent type: Ch White Rover of the Arctic, pictured on a cigarette card in the 1930s.

The Kennel Club Standard 1967

Compared with the few additions made during the first two-thirds of the century, this version represented a considerable expansion and clarification. In our view it is the most descriptive and we regret that it was later changed in the interests of making all British standards conform to a single pattern. Interestingly, at the time of writing this book, this is still the official version used in New Zealand; the New Zealand Kennel Club prefers to retain it.

The General Appearance section still retained much of the original wording, but there were significant additions to it; these are shown in italics. The remainder was considerably enlarged by the inclusion of more parts of the dog described separately and in detail.

Characteristics: The Samoyed is intelligent, alert, full of action, but above all displaying affection towards all mankind.

General Appearance: The Samoyed, being essentially a working dog, should be strong and active and graceful, and as his work lies in cold climates his coat should be heavy and weather-resisting. He should not be too long in back, as a weak back would make him practically useless for his legitimate work; but at the same time a cobby body, such as the Chow's, would also place him at a great disadvantage as a draught dog. Breeders should aim for the happy medium - viz, a body not long, but muscular, allowing liberty, with a deep chest and well-sprung ribs, *strong neck proudly arched, straight front and exceptionally strong loins. Both* *dogs and bitches should give the appearance of being capable of great endurance but should be free from coarseness.* A full grown dog should stand about 21in at the shoulder. On account of the depth of chest required, the legs should be moderately long; a very short-legged dog is to be deprecated. Hindquarters should be particularly well developed, *stifles well angulated,* and any suggestions of unsound stifles or cow hocks severely penalised.

Head and Skull: Head powerful and wedge-shaped with a broad, flat skull, muzzle of medium length, a tapering foreface not too sharply defined. Lips black, hair short and smooth before the ears. Nose black for preference, but may be brown or flesh-coloured. Strong jaws.

Eyes: Almond shaped, medium to dark brown in colour, set well apart with alert and intelligent expression. Eyerims should be black and unbroken.

Ears: Thick, not too long and slightly rounded at the tips, set well apart and well covered inside with hair. The ears should be fully erect in the grown dog.

Mouth: Upper teeth should just overlap the underteeth in a scissor bite.

Neck: Proudly arched.

Forequarters: Legs straight and muscular with good bone.

Body: Back medium in length, broad and very muscular. Chest broad and deep. Ribs well sprung, giving plenty of heart and lung room.

Hindquarters: Very muscular, stifles well angulated; cow hocks or straight stifles very objectionable.

Feet: Long, flattish and slightly spread out. Soles well cushioned with hair.

Tail: Long and profuse, carried over the back when alert; sometimes dropped when at rest.

Coat: The body should be well covered with a thick, close, soft and short undercoat, with harsh hair growing through it, forming the outer coat, which should stand straight away from the body and be free from curl.

Colour: Pure white; white and biscuit; cream.

Disposition: Alert and intelligent, showing marked affection towards all mankind. Unprovoked aggressiveness to be severely penalised.

Movement: Should move freely with a strong agile drive showing power and elegance.

Weight and Size: Dogs 20–22in at the shoulder. Bitches 18–20in at the shoulder. Weight in proportion to size.

Faults: Big ears with little feathering. Drop ears. Narrow width between ears. Long foreface. Blue or very light eyes. A bull neck. A long body. A soft coat; a wavy coat; absence of undercoat. Slack tail carriage; should be carried well over the back, though it may drop when the dog is at rest. Absence of feathering. Round, cat-like feet. Black or black spots. Severe unprovoked aggressiveness. Any sign of unsound movement.

The Scale of Points was dropped from all British standards at this revision.

CURRENT STANDARDS

The following are the current Standards published by The Kennel Club, the Fédération Cynologique Internationale (FCI) and the American Kennel Club (AKC).

The Kennel Club Breed Standard for the Samoyed

Reprinted by kind permission of The Kennel Club.

General Appearance: Most striking. Medium and well balanced. Strong, active, free from coarseness but capable of great endurance.

Characteristics: Intelligent, alert, full of action. 'Smiling expression'.

Temperament: Displays affection to all mankind. Unprovoked nervousness or aggression highly undesirable

Ch Snowmyth Mivara, top-winning bitch (24 CCs).

Head and Skull: Head powerful, wedge shaped, with broad flat skull, muzzle medium length, tapering foreface not too sharply defined. Lips black. Hair short and smooth before ears. Nose black for preference, but may be brown or flesh-coloured.

Eyes: Almond shaped, set slanted, medium to dark brown, set well apart with alert, intelligent expression. Eyerims unbroken black. Light or black eyes undesirable.

Ears: Thick, not too long, slightly rounded at tips, set well apart and well covered inside with hair. Fully erect in adults.

Mouth: Jaws strong with a perfect, regular and complete scissor bite, i.e. upper teeth closely overlapping the lower teeth and set square to the jaws.

Neck: Strong, not too short, and proudly arched.

Forequarters: Shoulders well laid, legs straight and muscular with good bone and not too short.

Body: Back medium in length, broad and very muscular with exceptionally strong loin. Chest deep but not too broad, well sprung ribs, giving plenty of heart and lung room.

Hindquarters: Very muscular, stifles well angulated, viewed from the rear legs straight and parallel with well let down hocks. Cow hocks or straight stifles highly undesirable.

Feet: Long, flattish, slightly spread and well feathered. Soles well cushioned with hair. Round cat feet highly undesirable.

Tail: Long, profusely coated, carried over the back and to side when alert, sometimes dropped when at rest.

Gait/Movement: Moves freely with strong, agile drive, showing power and elegance.

Coat: Body should be well covered with thick, close, soft and short undercoat, with harsh but not wiry hair growing through it,

Ch Zamoyski Lucky Star of Ostyak, BOB at Crufts 1987/1988, Working Group winner 1988.

forming weather resistant outer coat which should stand away from body and be free from curl.

Colour: Pure white, white and biscuit, cream, outer coat silver tipped.

Size: Dogs 51–56cm (20–22in) at shoulder. Bitches 46–51cm (18–20in) at shoulder. Weight in proportion to size.

Faults: Any departure from the foregoing points should be considered a fault and the seriousness with which the fault should be regarded should be in exact proportion to its degree.

Note: Male animals should have two apparently normal testicles fully descended into the scrotum.

The Samoyed Breed Standard of the Fédération Cynologique Internationale

Reprinted by kind permission of the FCI.

Country of Origin: Nordic countries.

The Samoyed

General Appearance: The Samoyed is a 'just off square' Arctic Spitz. Elegant in appearance, it presents a picture of strength, grace, agility, dignity and self-confidence.

Head: Strong, with wedge-shaped, slightly crowned skull. Well defined stop. Muzzle strong and deep, of about the same length as the skull, and tapering evenly to the nose. Bridge of the nose straight. Lips tight at cheeks and somewhat 'meaty'. Well developed nose. The mouth should be slightly curved up at the corners to form the 'Samoyed smile'.

Bite: Scissors bite*, pincer bite tolerated but undesirable.

Eyes: Dark brown, deep set with alert intelligent expression. Positioned well apart, slightly slanting and almond shaped.

Ears: Set high and well apart, relatively small, triangular, erect, mobile and slightly rounded at the tips.

Neck: Strong, moderately long and carried proudly erect.

Body: The body slightly longer than the height at the withers, deep and compact, but agile. Back of medium length, muscular and straight. Rich ruff. Bitches may be slightly longer in the back than males, very strong loins and moderate tuck up. Viewed from the front, the chest is broad and deep, but not barrelled. Well sprung ribs. Croup full, strong, muscular and slightly sloping.

Extremities: Well positioned and muscular with pronounced strong bone. Shoulders long, firm and sloping. Viewed from front, forelegs are straight and elbows close to the body. Pasterns strong but flexible. Hind legs viewed from the rear should be straight and parallel with very strong muscles. Stifles and hocks well angulated and hock joint low set. Dew claws should be removed when puppies are 3–4 days old.

Feet: Oval and springy, with toes slightly arched and slightly spread.

Movement: The Samoyed is a trotter. The gait should be free and vigorous with good reach in the forequarters, and good driving power in the hindquarters.

Tail: When alert and in movement the tail is carried bent forward over the back or side, but may be dropped when at rest, then reaching the hocks.

Coat: Well furred, heavy, flexible and dense. The Samoyed is a double coated dog, with short, soft, dense and close undercoat, and longer, straight and harsh

Annan Snow Eagle, aged 12 months, shows the Samoyed smile.

Sammyland Princess Jade at 12 months, with the results of outstanding success in Brazil.

hair growing through to form the outer coat. The coat should form a ruff around the neck and shoulders, framing the head, especially with males. On outside of ears and on head as well as front of legs, hair is short and smooth. Inside the ears should be well furred, and there should be a protective growth of hair between the toes. The tail should be profusely covered with hair. The coat of the female is often shorter and softer in texture than that of the male.

Colour: White, cream or white and biscuit. (The basic colour should be white with slight biscuit markings, and must never give the impression of being pale brown.) Nose, lips and eyerims are black. The nose sometimes liver with some loss of pigment.

Height: Ideal for males is 57cm ± 3, and for females 53 cm ± 3.

Serious Faults: Yellow eyes, flop ears, low build, light bones. Badly cow hocked. Wavy coat or long soft droopy coat, males which are not masculine and females which are not feminine. Double hook tail, reserved disposition.

Disqualifications: Eyes blue or of different colours. Overshot bite or undershot bite*. Colour of coat any other than permitted in Standard. Shy or aggressive disposition.

Note: Male animals should have two apparently normal testicles fully descended into the scrotum.

Comments on the standard for the Samoyed

Any deviation from the Standard is a fault and shall be judged in relation to the merits of the dog, general impression and constitution. Deviations which are atypical of the breed and abnormalities are disqualifying. See also Shows Regulations.

Bite: the bite includes not only teeth, but also jaws which should be well developed. The teeth formula is:

2 x 3 [incisors], 1 [canine], 4 [pre-molars], 2 [molars] upper jaw   = 42 teeth
2 x 3 [incisors], 1 [canine], 4 [pre-molars], 3 [molars] lower jaw

(NB – The FCI Standard includes diagrams illustrating the points marked *)

The American Kennel Club Standard for the Samoyed

Reprinted by kind permission of the American Kennel Club (dated 1997).

General Conformation

(a) General Appearance – The Samoyed, being essentially a working dog, should present a picture of beauty, alertness and strength, with agility, dignity and grace. As his work lies in cold climates, his coat should be heavy and weather resistant, well groomed, and of good quality rather than quantity. The male carries more of a 'ruff' than the female. He should not be long in the back as a weak back would make him useless for his legitimate work, but at the same time, a close-coupled body would also place him at a disadvantage as a draft dog. Breeders should aim for the happy medium, a body not long but muscular, allowing liberty, with a deep chest and well-sprung ribs, strong neck, straight front and especially strong loins. Males should be masculine in appearance and deportment without unwarranted aggressiveness; bitches should be feminine without weakness of structure or apparent softness of temperament. Bitches may be slightly longer in the back than males. They should both give the appearance of being capable of great endurance but be free from coarseness. Because of the depth of chest required, the legs should be moderately long. A very short legged dog is to be deprecated. Hindquarters should be particularly well developed, stifles well bent and any suggestion of unsound stifles or cow hocks severely penalized. General appearance should include movement and general conformation, indicating balance and good substance.

(b) Substance – Substance is that sufficiency of bone and muscle which rounds out a balance with the frame. The bone is heavier than would be expected in a dog of this size but is not so massive as to prevent the speed and agility most desirable in a Samoyed. In all builds, bone should be in proportion to body size. The Samoyed should never be so heavy as to appear clumsy nor so light as to appear racy. The weight should be in proportion to the height.

(c) Height – Males 21–23.5in; females 19–21in at the withers. An oversized or undersized Samoyed is to be penalized according to the extent of the deviation.

(d) Coat (Texture & Condition) – The Samoyed is a double-coated dog. The body should be well-covered with an undercoat of soft, short, thick, close wool with longer and harsh hair

growing through it to form the outer coat, which stands straight out from the body and should be free from curl. The coat should form a ruff around the neck and shoulders, framing the neck (more on males than on females). Quality of coat should be weather resistant and considered more than quantity. A droopy coat is undesirable. The coat should glisten with a silver sheen. The female does not usually carry as long a coat as most males and it is softer in texture.

(e) *Color* – Samoyeds should be pure white, white and biscuit, cream, or all biscuit. Any other colors disqualify.

Movement

(a) *Gait* – The Samoyed should trot, not pace. He should move with a quick agile stride that is well timed. The gait should be free, balanced and vigorous, with good reach in the forequarters and good driving power in the hindquarters. When trotting, there should be a strong rear action drive. Moving at a slow walk or trot, they will not single

John Moody mushing with a team of US and Canadian show champions in Idaho – as strong as they are beautiful.

track, but as speed increases the legs gradually angle inward until the pads are finally falling on a line directly under the longitudinal center of the body. As the pad marks converge the forelegs and hind legs are carried straight forward in traveling, the stifles are not turned in nor out. The back should remain strong, firm and level. A choppy or stilted gait should be penalized.

(b) *Rear End* – Upper thighs should be well developed. Stifles well bent – approximately 45 degrees to the ground. Hocks should be well developed, sharply defined and set at approximately 30 per cent of hip height. The hind legs should be parallel when viewed from the rear in a natural stance, strong, well developed, turning neither in nor out. Straight stifles are objectionable. Double jointedness or cowhocks are a fault. Cowhocks should only be determined if the dog has had an opportunity to move properly.

(c) *Front End* – Legs should be parallel and straight to the pasterns. The pasterns should be strong, sturdy and straight, but flexible with some spring for proper let-down of feet. Because of depth of chest, legs should be moderately long. Length of leg from the ground to the elbow should be approximately 55 per cent of the total height at the withers – a very short legged dog is to be deprecated. Shoulders should be long and sloping, with a lay-back of 45 degrees and be firmly set. Out at the shoulders or out at the elbow should be penalized. The withers' separation should be approximately 1.5in.

(d) Feet – Large, long, flattish – a hare-foot, slightly spread but not splayed; toes arched; pads thick and tough, with protective growth of hair between the toes. Feet should turn neither in nor out in a natural stance but may turn in slightly in the act of pulling. Turning out, pigeon-toed, round or cat-footed or splayed are faults. Feathers on feet are not too essential but are more profuse on females than males.

Head

(a) Conformation – Skull is wedge-shaped, broad, slightly crowned, not round or apple-headed, and should form an equilateral triangle on lines between the inner base of the ear and the center point of the stop. *Muzzle* – Muzzle of medium length and medium width, neither coarse nor snipey; should taper toward the nose and be in proportion to the size of the dog and the width of the skull. The muzzle must have depth. Whiskers are not to be removed. *Stop* – Not too abrupt, nevertheless well defined. *Lips* – Should be black for preference and slightly curved up at the corners of the mouth, giving the 'Samoyed smile'. Lip lines should not have the appearance of being coarse nor should the flews drop predominately at corners of the mouth. *Ears* – Strong and thick, erect, triangular and slightly rounded at the tips; should not be large or pointed, nor should they be small and 'bear eared'. Ears should conform to head size but be within the border of the outer edge of the head; they should be mobile and well covered inside with hair; hair full and stand off before the ears. Length of ear should be the same measurement as the distance from the inner base of ear to outer corner of eye. *Eyes* – Should be dark for preference; should be placed well apart and deep-set; almond shaped with lower lid slanting towards an imaginary point approximating the base of ears. Dark eye rims for preference. Round or protruding eyes penalized. Blue eyes disquali-fying. *Nose* – Black for preference but brown, liver, or Dudley nose not penalized. Color of nose sometimes changes with age and weather. *Jaws and teeth* – Strong, well set teeth, snugly overlapping with scissors bite. Undershot or overshot should be penalized.

(b) Expression – The expression, referred to as 'Samoyed expression', is very important and is indicated by sparkle of the eyes, animation and lighting up of the face when alert or intent on anything. Expression is made up of a combination of eyes, ears and mouth. The ears should be erect when alert; the mouth should be slightly curved up at the corners to form the 'Samoyed smile'.

Torso

(a) Neck – Strong, well muscled, carried proudly erect, set on sloping shoulders to carry head with dignity when at attention. Neck should blend into shoulders with a graceful arch.

(b) Chest – Should be deep, with ribs well sprung out from the spine and flattened at the sides to allow proper movement of the shoulders and freedom for the front legs. Should not be barrel-chested. Perfect depth of chest approximates the point of elbows, and the deepest part of the chest should be back of the forelegs – near the ninth rib. Heart and lung room are secured more by body depth than width.

(c) Loin and Back – The withers forms the highest part of the back. Loins strong and slightly arched. The back should be straight to the loin, medium in length, very muscular and neither

long nor short-coupled. The dog should be 'just off square' – the length being approximately 5 per cent more than the height. Females are allowed to be slightly longer than males. The belly should be well shaped and tightly muscled and, with the rear of the thorax, should swing up in a pleasing curve (tuck-up). Croup must be full, slightly sloping, and must continue imperceptibly to the tail root.

Samoyed Association of Canada Show 1974, judged by Irene Ashfield.
BOB: Ker-Lu's Bonnie Lassie.

Tail
The tail should be moderately long with the tail bone terminating approximately at the hock when down. It should be profusely covered with long hair and carried forward over the back or side when alert, but sometimes dropped when at rest. It should not be high or low set and should be mobile when loose – not tight over the hock. A double hook is a fault. A judge should see the tail over the back once when judging.

Disposition
Intelligent, gentle, adaptable, alert, full of action, eager to serve, friendly but conservative, not distrustful or shy, not overly aggressive. Unprovoked aggressiveness to be severely penalized.

Disqualifications
Any color other than pure white, cream, biscuit, or white and biscuit. Blue eyes.

CHAPTER **three**

Choosing a Puppy

If you are on the verge of deciding that a Samoyed is for you, try to see some adult dogs at a show or visit someone who owns one before you finally commit yourself. An adorable bundle of white fluff grows into a fairly strong medium sized dog – so be sure this is what you want.

The Samoyed 'smile'.

Do the profiles match?

In the business and service worlds much is made of the need to match personality and job profiles. It's very sensible to do the same with a prospective pet, so here is a checklist of the main Samoyed characteristics. If you are considering whether a Samoyed will suit you and your lifestyle, you may find it useful to check the following points against your circumstances and personality. This may help you to avoid getting a dog that does things you don't like, even though you may love its appearance. Alternatively, you'll know better from the beginning what your way of life is going to be if you decide to share your home with one... or two...

All dogs respond to situations and stimuli with conditioned reflex actions based on centuries of inheritance within their breeds, and the breeds largely were developed by humans for particular purposes. So each dog is true to its breed. Therefore you can't take a Samoyed, because you like its looks, then train it to behave like a Border Collie because you want it to respond implicitly to your every command. It won't. Don't buy an orange if you really want a banana.

The statements in italics describe features of very many Samoyeds. Beneath are some implications. If these give you some concern you should think about looking for a breed that better meets your requirements. But if you like most of the characteristics, a Samoyed will like you.

Definitely one of the family!

- *Samoyeds love human company.*

  Samoyeds don't do well if left alone for many hours.

- *Samoyeds bark to attract attention and show pleasure.*

  This can be quite loud. A single dog is not likely to bark often.

- *They are not guard dogs in the sense of defending property...*

  ...but they will bark to 'welcome' intruders!

- *Samoyeds like being, and expect to be, 'one of the family'.*

Puppies chew – anything.

Samoyeds don't do well if they are ignored or 'pushed out'.

- *Samoyeds like being active and really enjoy walks and free exercise.*

  Samoyeds cannot be fully fit if they have to lie around for most of their lives.

- *Samoyeds love to roam freely...*

  ... so at home they need some space and a well-fenced garden.

The Samoyed

- *Most Samoyeds dig sometimes.*
  Soft soil is a favourite.
- *Samoyed puppies chew when teeth are growing.*
  They need appropriate toys during this stage.
- *They are independent to an extent and have individual natures.*
  No two Samoyeds are exactly the same.
- *They can be trained to be socially acceptable and biddable...*
  ... but most will decide to 'do their own thing' occasionally.
- *They learn easily.*
  They easily pick up habits you don't want them to have as well as the ones you do.
- *Samoyeds' coats need some grooming.*
  They need brushing and combing to look their best.
- *Occasionally, Samoyeds get dirty.*
  When they do, they need bathing.
- *Coats are shed – usually once a year, sometimes twice in warm houses, and a bitch sheds after having puppies.*
  When this happens mounds of fur are shed.
- *Many Samoyeds have innate herding instincts.*
  Samoyeds won't hurt animals they herd, but farmers don't know this.
- *Most will chase small animals, for instance rabbits.*

This bitch has always loved (digging up) potted plants.

Many Samoyeds have innate herding instincts – so be careful if your puppy meets sheep!

'Any chance of squeezing in one more?'

This applies when out on walks; they will live with these at home.
- *They will happily live with cats in the household...*
  ... but they may chase ones belonging to neighbours.
- *Most Samoyeds are healthy.*
  Due to increased popularity a few inherited problems have appeared recently.
- *You should never hit a Samoyed.*
  It rarely associates punishment with something it has done.
- *Samoyeds become a 'way of life'.*
  Most people who have lived with a Samoyed find they must have another when it dies.

Where to obtain your Samoyed

The next consideration is likely to be from where to obtain a puppy. We strongly advise that you try to find a reputable breeder who, because he or she exhibits stock regularly, wants to breed the very best both in terms of appearance and health. We do not advise buying from puppy farms or pet shops; you will know nothing of the background of the puppy and therefore unseen health problems may surface with consequent disappointment and expense.

Lists of breeders are available from various sources. You can telephone or write to The Kennel Club and ask for names of Samoyed breeders. The address is: The Kennel Club, 1–5 Clarges Street, Piccadilly, London W1Y 8AB. Telephone: 0171 493 6651, 6629 or 5828.

You will also find breeders advertising in the weekly dog papers, *Dog World and Our Dogs*. Avoid advertisements placed in non-specialist papers. Alternatively, you may know someone who shows dogs – it doesn't matter which breed – whom you can ask to put you in touch with breeders of Samoyeds, or with the secretary of one of the breed clubs.

When you find some breeders, ask about prices and availability. You may have to wait, so be prepared to do this. Don't expect to find a well-reared puppy the moment you want one. Good ones don't come 'off the peg'.

When the time comes to select you may wish to enlist the help of an experienced breeder or a knowledgeable friend who will go with you, especially if you intend to show. Making the final choice is by no means easy. We have done this on many occasions for friends and then followed the dogs' subsequent careers in the show ring with fingers firmly crossed! We confess to a glow of satisfaction when they win well or even become champions.

Dog or bitch?

You should decide whether you particularly want a dog or a bitch, or whether you have no strong preference. In some breeds bitches tend to be more affectionate, but with Samoyeds that difference is hardly noticed. In the words of the Breed Standard, the breed *displays affection to all mankind.*

Obviously, bitches have seasons. Samoyed bitches don't usually attract male dogs from all round the neighbourhood, but they may well take a lively interest in any they see.

Two-way communication at the Astutus Pet Hotel.

Dogs are very strong and carry heavier coats. They may be attracted to females of other breeds living near you and wander off to visit them if you don't have an adequately fenced garden.

A show puppy?

The breeder may well ask you whether you want to show. Some people think this implies the breeder will dump a poor specimen on the inexperienced purchaser who says no. This certainly will not be the case if you have chosen the breeder carefully – someone whose stock is well known or is gaining a reputation. The point behind the question is that, if you are going to show, the breeder wants to select a puppy that is likely to do better in the show ring than others. The breeder will be delighted if you succeed.

If you don't want to show there should be no less value in a healthy, lively puppy in the same litter that does not have the same show potential. Often the difference is marginal: slightly larger ears, or possibly a slightly softer coat. Away from the show ring such Samoyeds are just as good, just as healthy and certainly just as lovable and loving as all the rest. Every litter will have a mixture.

Parents and grandparents

Most strongly we advise that you should try to see both parents before deciding you will have a puppy from a particular litter. If you intend to show we suggest you find out as much as you can and see, if at all possible, the four grandparents as well.

Quite probably you will be able to see some of them at a show. Don't judge their standard from how well or otherwise they do at one show. Although all judges work to the same breed standard they give differing interpretations. Talk to people about the breeding you have in mind, but use your common sense – not every person readily discusses his or her dog's faults.

Above all, look hard at the grandparents and parents to see how similar, or otherwise, they appear. If they are similar they are said to be 'of a type' and it is most likely that the puppies will be fairly similar. However, if most of the six antecedents look rather different from one another, there is more likely to be a mixture of type amongst the puppies. Probably they will inherit appearance from the most dominant individual, which is just as likely to be a bitch as a dog.

The crucial point is to decide whether you like what you see. If you find you are disappointed in the two previous generations, don't be fooled into imagining that those lovely white bundles you are considering will be miraculously different. With the inevitability of the ages they will follow their inheritance.

A point to bear in mind when you see the dam with her litter is that she will shed her coat some weeks after giving birth. If you have taken our advice and seen her well beforehand you will know her normal appearance. Bitches vary as to when the post-whelping shed occurs; the season and temperature have an effect on the timing as well.

Family likeness, with father in the centre and mother (badly out of coat after whelping) on the right.

Which one?

When the puppies are at your feet, scampering hither and thither, you can be forgiven for asking, 'How on earth can you tell them apart?' With a cursory glance they all seem identical. However, if you spend an hour or so with them you will soon begin to see differences. One may be the imp which is truly into everything – pulling at your shoes, jumping on the others, grabbing the odd ear as a sibling passes, or racing to the door if someone comes in.

Soon you will begin to spot some differences in shape as well, probably because there are variations in weight. Sometimes this is simply a difference between dogs and bitches, but at this age you can have lighter dogs and heavier bitches, depending on what they eat. Some Samoyeds are greedy while others are more fastidious, even as young puppies.

If you have decided you want a dog and the litter has both dogs and bitches, have only the dogs in view when you are making your selection, or vice versa. This eases the task of selection by excluding distractions.

You should certainly choose a confident puppy. Avoid one that does not take part in the

'Which do you think is "pick of the litter"?'
Beryl Grounds with Sarah Styles, Hilary Breeze and 'babies'.

general tumbling and chasing typical of a lively, healthy litter. Then pick them up, one at a time, holding each puppy in one hand with your first finger between the front legs, your thumb on one side and the remaining fingers on the other. The puppy then is lying securely and comfortably in the palm of your hand.

The body should feel warm, reasonably firm and pliable. Its tummy should not feel bulging and tight unless it has just eaten; if it has this is not the best time to be looking at the litter. An otherwise tight tummy could suggest worms or a digestive problem. Then consider its coat quality. With your other hand, run your fingers between its fur and up towards its head. This should feel fairly dense and close and not too soft or silky. The hairs should stand straight out from its body and there shouldn't be any curl.

The puppy should be quite content to be held like this and indeed should like the contact. Inevitably, it will become bored after a time and want to play again, so let it go and pick it up again later for further inspection.

Checking the main breed points

What follows is advice on making your selection with a view to showing your puppy. It is reasonably comprehensive because new breeders who have litters may also want help in deciding which puppy to keep for show.

Eyes: With a puppy in your hand, turn it to face you and look carefully at the head. From a health point of view you don't want any discharge from the inner corners of the eyes giving brown lines down the muzzle. This can be present for various reasons (see chapter 7).

For showing, look at the eye shape, colour, and surrounding pigment. The shape should not be unduly round; the correct shape is that of an almond. The outer corner of the eye should be pointing towards the outer base of the puppy's ear. This is an important pointer to attractive balance in the adult's expression. At six weeks the eye colour is blue/grey and this should darken to brown later. Look at the circle of pigment surrounding the iris. This shouldn't be a light shade; if it is the adult eye will be light brown or yellowish/orange in colour. The pigment of the eyerim should be 'black' by six weeks, unbroken by any pink sections. If there are any it is unlikely they will completely fill in later.

Zamoyski Lucky Valentine of Amarige as a puppy...

Ears: Shortly after birth puppies' ears are folded downwards, but fairly soon they begin to strengthen and finally become erect. At six weeks they are usually still folded but are beginning to firm up at the base. For showing, adult ears that are not too large are preferred, set well apart but facing forward.

Deciding which puppy has the best ear set is not easy until you have handled many and watched them grow up. Put your finger and thumb between the ears and judge the width of the skull, and then do the same with the other puppies and see whether you can spot differences. Probably you will distinguish between dogs and bitches first, but you may also be able to spot variations between others. They will be slight at this stage, but heads enlarge considerably.

Look at the puppy directly from the front again and try to

... and as an adult dog.

see whether the folded ears are facing directly towards you or more at an angle. The ones facing forward are more likely to do the same when erect as an adult. Puppies are adept at swivelling their ears, so you have to assess the set when they are reasonably relaxed; for instance, when they are sitting but not lying down.

Mouth: You must look at a puppy with its mouth closed as well as open. The open mouth should show black pigment around the lips. At six weeks it is possible there could be still some smallish section not yet filled in. If this is the case probably it will complete. If large sections are still pink then parts of these are most likely to remain. Pigment is certainly controlled by heredity factors.

The open mouth should show black pigment around the lips.

An important point to look for in a puppy's face is the typical 'smile'. In an adult this should be seen with the mouth closed as well as open. When closed and viewed from the side the lips extend from the front of the jaw and along the side, finishing in a distinct upward turn towards the eye. Some, however, have heavy lips which droop downward at the side. It isn't easy to spot this heaviness in a puppy so you should assess the lips of the parents and grandparents.

Teeth at this stage will be the small first set, but how they are placed is a good guide to the adult mouth. Puppies are not at all co-operative in the matter of having their bite examined, when you try to look at their front teeth with the mouth closed but the lips parted. However, if you're going to show, the pup has to get used to the process, so persevere, but be gentle. The young teeth should be even, with the incisors very slightly overlapping; in other words, the upper front ones touching the lower ones just in front in the required scissor bite. Don't choose a puppy whose front teeth are at all over- or undershot. Such a mouth is most unlikely to improve.

Head: Finally, judge the puppies' heads as entities, not just as the sum of the parts. Get someone to hold them two at time, side by side. Look at the overall shape of the skull, the

space between the ears, the width between the eyes, the way the puppy looks forward at you, the length of the muzzle, the bones beneath the eyes. Compare and contrast.

We can't tell you finally and precisely how to decide which has, and will have, the best head and expression, or whether the particular litter you are looking at has a worthwhile one at all. However, if you want to show, the more you do this, then watch how the puppies develop and how they appear as adults, the more you will hone your skill.

Front: Feel the puppy's legs with your thumb and first finger and check that the bones are straight. If you can watch from the front as the puppy trots towards you, see whether the front legs reach well forward as it moves. This is desirable because it suggests the puppy will have good extension in the forelegs as an adult.

Another important point to look for in the front is the width between the legs across the chest. This should be about one-and-a-half fingers, though that's inevitably a rather vague guide. It is another of the very many points in a Samoyed where you want

**Development of a champion:
Ch Fairvilla Aga Khan as a puppy (top)
and as an adult dog (above).**

neither too much nor too little. A very small gap between the legs suggests a narrow chest, whereas too much suggests the beginnings of a barrel – and both are wrong.

Body: Look at and feel the shoulder and chest, having checked a clear drawing of the Samoyed skeleton. You need to feel the beginnings of the curve from near the spine down to the breastbone where the ribs join. The sides should not be flat but should have a gentle curve which will develop into the correct rib cage when adult.

Feel the puppy's neck. An adult looks best if it has a really good arch from the spine up to the back of the skull; therefore the puppy should have adequate length of neck for this to develop. You can see this if you are looking sideways on and the puppy is alert and attracted to something a distance away and slightly upwards.

Feel the underside of the puppy from the breastbone to between the back legs. This needs to extend in a graceful curve in the adult – it's known as the 'tuck-up'. It won't be so obvious in a puppy, but nevertheless you should be able to see it partially. The point to look for is whether there is a good depth of the chest at the front.

The spine finishes in the tail. How this is 'set on' is most important to the appearance of the adult. Ideally there should be a straight, level spine with the tail curving back directly towards the head. Check that the tail is straight right along its length. Since it is the continuation of the spine there should be no suggestion of a kink.

Sasoolka I Love Trouble looking entirely innocent as a puppy.

Then look at the rear legs. From the side there should be a good angulation of the stifle. This means that, when the puppy is standing still and his hocks are upright, there is a very distinct slope at the front of the leg up to the hip. This angle is important in helping the adult move with strong drive in the rear legs.

Rear: When the puppy moves away from you in a straight line you should see the legs swinging forwards and backwards in a straight line from the hips, just as with the front legs from the shoulders. Puppies scamper all over the place, so you have to be patient, but

Sasoolka I Love Trouble with a wicked grin at 12 months old.

sooner or later you'll be able to check this. It really is important, because often you can see adult Samoyeds with incorrect movement. Some of this, undoubtedly, is due to wrong exercise or lack thereof, but some of it is due to heredity. Again, this is something to look at closely in the parents and grandparents.

We wish we could give you a foolproof way of spotting which puppies are likely to have well-formed hips with hardly any suggestion of dysplasia (see chapter 7) or, better still, none at all. We can't, and no specialist will interpret an X-ray plate until the dog is a year old. Certainly you should consider the hip scores of the parents and grandparents.

CHAPTER
four
Getting it Right from the Start

If you have just brought your puppy home, no doubt you are pleased and excited at the prospect of developing a happy relationship with it. Assuredly you will, with some sensible care and attention. This chapter covers various aspects of responsible ownership, but it starts by considering food – the first item on the puppy's agenda!

Feeding your new puppy

A responsible breeder will give you some of the puppy's normal food and a diet sheet. You should keep to this diet as closely as possible to avoid digestive upsets. Complete foods are available and suppliers offer different kinds according to age. Some owners feed this kind of food exclusively, others feel that meals they make up are better, such as canned puppy food or minced meat and biscuit, interspersed with milk-based meals such as creamed rice.

'Is it dinner time yet?'

In the past we used to feed our adult dogs on raw meat or cooked tripe and biscuit. We gradually prepared our puppies for this by giving them scraped beef, then moving on to mince and then small pieces as they grew. Many people now use canned puppy food and biscuit, mainly because it is more convenient. Whichever you choose, the important point is that the puppy receives a properly balanced diet with correct but not overdone vitamins. If you want to make up meals we suggest the following four meals each day:

1   Cereals and biscuit, or crushed cereal such as Weetabix or Farex in about 200ml (1/3 pint) of milk.
2   115–140g (4–5oz) finely-minced meat and soaked biscuit + half the daily vitamin supplement (for example, Canovel or SA 37).
3   As for 2, though the meat can be replaced by other protein such as a scrambled egg, fish, rabbit or chicken.
4   A milky meal, such as tinned creamed rice, with biscuit or crushed cereal.

This is a good diet for puppies. However, it is expensive, so some breeders give one fresh meat meal and canned food for the other meat meal, so that the puppy is used to both when it changes home.

The meals should be fairly well spaced out through the day. You'll want to combine feeding with the beginning of house training (see page 60), so after each meal you must take the puppy outside and wait for it to 'perform'. You won't want to do this late at night, so the fourth meal may well be supper at about 9.00 pm. As he grows older and meals are reduced, this can be the first to be dropped, usually at about 12 weeks of age.

Normally, your puppy will let you know how much food to give. When there is no competition from litter-mates a single dog usually eats what it requires and leaves the rest. The puppy also will indicate when to reduce the number of meals. When it toys with one it's probably time to leave it out and spread the others over the day. By about 12 months of age, the dog should require only one meal a day. Some dogs are greedier than others, and you should not let a puppy become too heavy. Exercise plays a part, and a dog with a very active lifestyle will probably develop a very healthy appetite.

As a guide, a puppy about four months old should reach about half its weight as an adult, so if you weigh it regularly and know what this is, you have a marker against which you can measure later development. To weigh the dog, pick it up and stand on the bathroom scales. Reading the display may require a partner; probably you'll have your face buried in a wriggling bundle of fur. Then weigh yourself and do the subtraction.

What you have taken on

There is advice about your puppy's first night in chapter 5, as well as how to get it used to its new existence, in which it is now completely dependent upon you, away from its mother and litter-mates. You, or someone else, needs to be on hand for most of the first fortnight if you expect your puppy to develop into a well-behaved, content and sociable dog. Even after that you should not be out for more than an hour or two until the puppy is four months old. You should regard having a puppy as comparable to looking after a young child.

In your home you should become the 'leader of the pack'. A puppy trained properly early in its life accepts the human as its leader and learns to respect and obey that leader.

If your puppy has a bout of diarrhoea, regard this as a warning sign that needs investigation. If it occurs very shortly after you bring the puppy home probably it is due to the change to the water in your area, and maybe because you are feeding it on different food from what it has had before. Check what you are giving the pup; offal such as liver can produce diarrhoea and rough biscuit or meal may do the same. Your puppy may have eaten something outside, so watch it carefully. If you are in doubt, or the diarrhoea seems severe or doesn't clear up within a day, consult your veterinary surgeon.

As your puppy grows it will lose its baby teeth. At this time its gums will become sore as the adult ones grow and you must expect it to chew things. Ensure that the pup can only get its teeth into what is safe, cannot be swallowed – and is acceptable to you!

Vaccination

Most vets start to vaccinate when the puppy is about eight weeks old. As soon as you have your puppy, decide which vet you are going to use and enquire about vaccination, because it does vary with area and degree of risk. When you visit for the first injections your vet will also carry out a health check which should include listening for any heart murmurs or other signs of illness. If you bought your puppy from a responsible breeder this will already have been done by another vet, whose name may be on the information sheets given to you.

Puppies have some immunity from disease passed to them from their dam in the colostrum, which is the first milk she produces and is, therefore, their first drink in the world. This can only be absorbed by the puppies on the first day or so after birth, but the protection lasts for six to eight weeks.

The four most important diseases from which your dog needs protection are: canine distemper, infectious canine hepatitis, leptospirosis and canine parvovirus. There is also kennel cough, and your vet may decide to vaccinate against this at the same time. The difference is that kennel cough vaccine is given by insertion into the nasal passages. Your puppy will need annual booster injections against these diseases. If at any time you put your dog into boarding kennels, reputable establishments will want to see up-to-date vaccination certificates.

The beginning of a love affair.

Leaving your Samoyed alone

You will want to know in greater detail the particular characteristics and temperament you can expect in your Samoyed as it grows. Already it should be clear that the core of your Sam's being is a love of people. As has been explained in chapter 1, this feature has been developed in the breed over many centuries. It follows that Samoyeds are not happy when deprived of human companionship for long periods. With this in mind, consider the situation when a dog has to sleep on its own at night, sees its owner for a short time during a hurried breakfast, is let out into the garden for a quarter of an hour or so, and then returned to a kitchen or kennel, to wait on his own from 8.00 am to 6.00 pm. Some evenings, when the owner stays in, the dog will get some four or five hours companionship if it's allowed in the same room, and maybe a walk as well, but no doubt there'll be evenings when the owner dashes out again and the dog is left companionless.

Now there are breeds that tolerate such a level of isolation, but the Samoyed most certainly will not. It is its nature to try to make the best of circumstances, so left to its own devices the Samoyed searches for something to do. Equipped with paws and teeth for a high proportion of its activities, it's small wonder that it tries to chew whatever is on hand, or digs. Moreover, it seems that when a Sam has done something twice it's learnt it for good. This is fine if you're trying to teach something useful, but sometimes it learns most quickly and effectively the very things you don't want it to do. It follows that, if it starts damaging things when left on its own, you may find it difficult to change the habit.

If you and the rest of the family are out for most of the day, you need to arrange that one of you returns at midday for a short while. This ensures the dog is not left alone for more than four or at most five hours at a stretch. Apart from the obvious need to relieve itself the dog needs some fun and activity for half an hour or so at lunch time, after which it will be quite content to settle down again for the afternoon. You need to train your Sam this way as a puppy, gradually increasing the time you leave it from an hour or so to three or four. Once it gets the message that you always return after not too long, it will be content to wait – although it would prefer you not to go at all.

Fortunately, a Samoyed is perfectly happy for anyone to appear, so you can arrange for a friend to visit at midday instead of you. This is why they are not good guard dogs: a burglar is first and foremost a human being to a Samoyed, whatever you may feel. The Samoyed may bark in vociferous welcome, which will be useful in such circumstances, but no-one will be able to tell the difference from its normal greeting, because there won't be any!

The length of time Sams can be left doesn't alter if there is more than one. They enjoy the companionship of others, but this is no substitute for human love and affection. Rather the propensity for mischief is increased if you condemn two or three to boring isolation.

Be warned! If you cannot avoid being out all day and there is no possibility of a regular midday visitor, you shouldn't choose a Samoyed, despite all its appealing features. Remember the adage, *You can't go against nature.* Samoyeds' love of people is centuries-old nature.

Health

Responsible owners watch their dogs' health carefully. Fortunately, given proper diet and exercise the great majority of carefully-bred Samoyeds live healthy and active lives. Visits to your vet are likely to be for routine matters.

However, if something is wrong the owner is the most likely person to spot the fact. Observe your dog sensibly and, when you feel all is not well, go to your vet and explain your concern as carefully as possible. This is a two-way affair: the vet wants to be confident in your judgement about your dog's behaviour, and you want to be confident that he or she will listen carefully and carry out all necessary tests if the reason is not obvious. Do try to build up this relationship. Your vet will not have many Samoyeds on the books so you will soon be recognised at the practice. Forge a partnership that benefits your dog when the need arises.

For one reason or another, any dog may have the occasional lengthy bout of ill health or meet with an accident. To be on the safe side it is sensible to take out insurance cover that includes part or full payment of veterinary fees. Specialist insurance companies such as Dog Breeders' Insurance, PetPlan and Pet Healthcare Insurance advertise in the dog press.

Legal responsibilities

Owners are required by The Environmental Protection Act (1990) to ensure that their dogs do not cause what is called a Statutory Noise Nuisance by their barking. People can make complaints to their local Environmental Health Department about any loud and continued noise; music and barking dogs constitute the majority of such complaints. Evidence is sought as to the length of time and/or severity of the barking given the particular environment, so there could be considerable difference between what causes a nuisance in a block of flats compared with among scattered buildings in the country. Owners of Samoyeds would be well advised to ensure that their dogs are not allowed to bark for long periods when outside.

There will be local bye-laws where you live relating to fouling of footpaths by dogs. Whenever you walk on public roads and footpaths you should be prepared to clear up after your dog. This means being equipped with a plastic bag and learning the trick of picking up faeces with it: drop a tissue on top, hand inside the bag, grab, turn the bag inside out and tie off to seal. Then dispose of it properly.

When being exercised on a public road a dog must be on a lead. A dog must also carry an identity disc on its collar with the owner's name and address indelibly marked upon it.

An owner of a dog that causes a traffic accident is legally responsible. You are strongly advised to take out appropriate third party insurance cover. This is sometimes part of a club's membership subscription, part of home contents insurance, or can be part of a general canine policy.

Dogs should not be allowed to run free with livestock in fields. Samoyeds may well try to herd and, although no normal one would ever harm animals it was herding, farmers rarely know the breed. Unfortunately, they are within their rights to shoot dogs, and some Samoyeds have met this fate although they were following their instinctive and caring heredity.

General care of your Samoyed

The kind of life you give your dog is the clue to how responsible an owner you are. This means thinking about your Sam as a dog, not as a human being. Most dogs sleep a large portion of their lives; when not active they will usually doze. So think about where your dog is going to do this, day and night.

If you keep your dog in the house, which it will prefer, organise accordingly. Dogs are creatures of habit. Think carefully before you decide that you'll let it sleep in your bedroom. Samoyeds shared humans' communal life in Siberia, which is why they'll happily share your bed, but your lifestyle is somewhat different. You may later have another dog, perhaps a third... do you want your bedroom to become a grandiose kennel?

If you decide to have kennels and runs, think about the level of interest, or lack of it,

**'What's good enough for the boss
is good enough for us!'**

there'll be for your dog. Make sure you take your dog out to do other things quite frequently. Make sure there are different surfaces for your Sam to lie upon; it will decide upon a favourite, but will change occasionally, perhaps because of the temperature. If your dog is confined at night make sure there is sufficient room, ventilation, warmth in winter and coolness in summer. Samoyeds can tolerate cold, dry weather, but that doesn't mean freezing conditions are ideal for them. They can and do develop arthritis and other joint problems later in life.

You may or may not love gardening, but most people like their gardens to be reasonably tidy. Some Samoyeds have a propensity for helping to organise gardens in a quite different way – and they can be remarkably strong diggers. You can work a compromise, especially if you decide to keep a number of them, by having

**Despite its Arctic origins, the Samoyed does not thrive
without a warm, dry place to sleep in.**

reasonably extensive runs along one side of the garden in which they can play quite happily. Then have them in the garden to play when you are there, or working in it.

Feeding is another matter for sensible consideration. A dog's digestive system has developed over thousands of years in response to having lumps of meat in the stomach, probably once a day. In that they are similar to many other creatures. The typical feeds we now use are somewhat different, but the once-a-day rule still applies in most circumstances while the dog is healthy.

In our opinion humans and dogs should eat separately, largely because if a dog is nearby it will try to cadge tidbits and most humans will respond. Once that happens a routine has been established and the dog will probably get extra and possibly unsuitable food regularly. Naturally, it will put on weight. An overweight Samoyed, like an undernourished one, is

pitiable. It will become unhealthy and unlikely to live to a ripe age.

Psychology – canine and human

The tendency to feed 'extras' to dogs often starts when they are used as substitute children. Many people remain single, and anyway, children depart in the fullness of time. If a dog comes into the house for the very natural reason of companionship, don't overdo things and treat it as a human. We know that very close bonds can and do develop, but nevertheless a dog remains a dog,

reacting to every moment as it happens. It cannot think as you do. A Samoyed may be capable of responding to some 30 or so words of command when fully trained for a specific purpose but don't let yourself say of your dog, 'He understands every word I say to him.' He does not, and cannot. Human and canine minds are very different. Everything a dog does is a response to a stimulus.

One facet of Samoyed behaviour occasionally is

Samoyeds excel in some activities: (top) the tunnelling expert, (above) the 'singer'.

misinterpreted. The Samoyed 'smile' is well known and a natural feature of a properly-formed face and muzzle. A few Sams take enjoyment one stage further; they actually lift a lip slightly, almost into a 'laugh'. On rare occasions, a Sam has 'laughed' in this way while playing and then become totally confused when its human companions have shied away – even reacted as though their canine friend were no longer trustworthy. As you can imagine, the dog's instincts give conflicting messages. Owners should understand that, if they have bought a Sam from good breeding lines where temperament is exemplary, as it should be, the dog will not react warningly while playing.

Another point of which owners should be aware in the matter of 'signals' is that quite a number of Sams feel they are so much part of the family they try to join in conversations. To do this they 'talk' with a sound that is neither a bark nor a howl, but a quieter mixture. Usually it is done with a slight lift of the head, as though the dog is going to howl but doesn't get that far. It is really quite engaging and if you answer similarly, you can set up quite a chat – though someone watching nearby may think you're going mad. It isn't at all like a growl.

Samoyeds with children

The fact that the dogs had to be so gentle in their companions' tents in Siberia doesn't mean you can let children mistreat Samoyeds with impunity. Responsible dog ownership means

'Who says dogs can't climb trees?'

training your children into responsible dog ownership. Children should never interfere with a dog when it is asleep. The dog also should be allowed to eat its food without interruption and preferably on its own.

Children must be taught not to get a dog too excited, not to handle puppies roughly, and not to praise them one minute only to get cross later as their own moods change. Typically, youngsters can be happy, excited, cross, loving, tired, all within an hour. Not so a dog.

Very young children should not be allowed to pick up a puppy, because they can easily drop it when it wriggles. Such a drop can cause unseen damage that may only come to light later in life. It is far better to accept a child's momentary disappointment.

Active, perhaps boisterous, youngsters should not play roughly with a puppy, even though it may give every sign of thoroughly enjoying the romp. Treating a puppy this way trains it in that form of behaviour. When it has grown to adult size a year later, a dog playing roughly can pose quite a problem, not least to the youngsters themselves.

Children should learn to keep their toys out of reach because puppies tend to pick up anything they come across. They should not get cross with a puppy that has run off with a toy or slipper left lying on the floor. Parents may find this an excellent reason to put forward to encourage clearing up.

You should not let children take out Samoyeds on their own. The dogs are very strong and pull naturally, so can easily get out of the control of a youngster, or indeed anyone who is not physically strong.

The interaction between Sams and children can provide a deeper level of love and affection within the family group, but to attain it takes moderate care. You'll need to give thoughtful attention to both.

The Kennel Club Good Citizen Dog Scheme

This scheme aims to produce a dog that will walk and sit in a controlled manner on the lead, lie down on command and allow the owner to clean and groom it and inspect its feet. The dog must also stand and lie down on either side or on its back, all on the lead. The dog must come to hand when called.

There are some nine exercises involved in the test. If the dog passes all of them a certificate is issued. Dogs can be entered at any age provided they have finished their vaccination programmes. The scheme is aimed at all, whether registered with The Kennel Club or not.

You may decide quite early on that you will set this as a target for your Samoyed to reach. If it does you will have proof that both of you have forged an excellent and responsible partnership.

The breed clubs

Once you have decided that the Samoyed really is the dog for you, you may wish to know more about breed affairs. First, you may wish to join one or more club. In Great Britain there are four devoted to Samoyeds:

* The Samoyed Association, founded in 1920
* The British Samoyed Club, founded in 1932
* The Northern Samoyed Society, founded in 1961
* The Samoyed Breeders and Owners League, founded in 1980

Each club organises its quota of shows allowed by The Kennel Club, normally one championship and one open. The Samoyed Association and the Samoyed Breeders and Owners League have Scottish branches and shows are regularly organised by them in Scotland. Each club organises breed stalls for the sale of a wide range of items of Samoyed interest: jewellery, pictures, ceramics, garments, dog accoutrements and, in the case of the Samoyed Association, its book, *The Samoyed*. These are mounted at their shows and at the ringside at Crufts.

The Breed Council

The Kennel Club prefers breeds to operate breed councils, though it does not require them to do so. The existence of a council facilitates The Kennel Club's communications in various matters, the most regular of which is consultation about the first appointments of judges to award Kennel Club Challenge Certificates (CCs). A Samoyed Breed Council was first formed in 1966, later discontinued, but then reconstituted.

A Breed Liaison Officer is appointed for a three-year period. Each club may put forward a name for this office and, in the event of several nominations, each club committee votes. Since 1991 the Breed Council has formally accepted that it operates within Kennel Club rules. Beryl has held this office since 1986.

The Council has no executive power over the breed clubs and exists as a forum for discussion and to arrange joint projects. There has been very considerable cooperation between the four clubs in various matters, particularly in the drawing up of the Code of Ethics (see Appendix A) and the qualifications for names to be added to judging lists (see chapter 12, page 176).

Examples of matters of general interest and concern to the breed discussed by the Breed Council are items from The Kennel Club requiring whole-breed consideration, the organisation of breed information displays such as Discover Dogs at Crufts and elsewhere, and the organisation of health seminars. In addition, subjects for discussion by the Council may be sent from any one or all of the breed clubs, or any individual Samoyed owner can write to it via the Breed Liaison Officer on a matter of general importance to the breed.

Rescue arrangements

Many breeds have devoted people who organise rescue schemes, and ours is no exception. Each of the clubs has a volunteer Rescue Officer and each organises social events to provide financial help in certain circumstances as sanctioned by the committee. Undoubtedly, a number of Samoyeds have to change homes because of unforeseen changes in owners' personal circumstances. Unfortunately, there are also some who have the misfortune to be taken on by owners who have no real commitment to them and tire quickly.

Rehoming a Samoyed is not undertaken lightly. Fortunately, many people are genuinely interested in providing a better home, or an equally good one, for a dog that has to change families. To minimise the possibility of yet a further change a new prospective owner is vetted as thoroughly as possible.

Because Samoyeds are so friendly towards their human partners the vast majority of owners give them worthy, contented and healthy homes for their full span of years.

Samoyed clubs in the United States of America

There are 30 or so independent regional clubs affiliated to the national organisation, the Samoyed Club of America (SCA) – the total varies slightly over time. One or two of these are devoted solely to rescue. The SCA was inaugurated at the Westminster Show in February 1923. It is controlled by a Board of Governors and currently has 14 standing committees or coordinators to organise such elements of its activities as Judges' Education, Awards, Independent Club Liaison, Club Historian and Budget.

There is one National Specialty for which the SCA invites bids annually. The country is divided into five regions for this purpose: 1 East, 2 West, 3 Central, 4 South, and 5 Northwest. The Specialty is normally held in each region in turn. The rota currently approved puts the 1997 Specialty in Region 1, continuing through to the Northwest in 2001. Applicants to host the Specialty may be a single regional club, two or more clubs acting together, or a group of individual SCA members.

The SCA produces an excellent large format magazine, *The Samoyed Bulletin*, which has gained publication awards. This carries a varied range of articles, some of which are reproduced from time to time as significant items of breed history, health matters or research. It also carries a large range of advertisements with pictures of stock.

We have been members of the SCA for a long time and our back copies of *The Samoyed Bulletin* provide a visual picture of the similarities and contrasts in the breed between Great Britain and the United States during the last 25 years. It is interesting for owners on both sides of the Atlantic to assess the changes in their respective branches of the breed from its common Siberian ancestors.

Samoyeds world-wide – the Internet

Increasingly, Samoyed owners are communicating globally with one another via the Internet. At the time of writing the following sites are of interest:

- **The Samoyed Club of America Homepage**
  http://www.samoyed.org/Samoyed_Club_of_America.html
  This comprehensive site includes the names and addresses of most Samoyed clubs world-wide.

- **Samfans**
  This off-line 'chat' area has contributors all over the world. To subscribe (free), go to:
  http://www.sdsmt.edu/other/dogs/groups/working/samoyed/samoyed.html

- **K9NetUK**
  This is a United Kingdom only site where breeders can advertise kennels for a fee:
  http://www.k9netuk.com/index.html

CHAPTER
five

Training

Everyone wants a dog to be well trained, but what people expect of their dogs varies enormously. We have pointed out the general characteristics of Samoyeds, and any training programme has to take account of these. For success in training Samoyeds you must understand what you are starting with: a dog happiest in human company, keen to please and be part of the family, expecting some independence, intelligent enough to see the easiest way, with average sight and sense of smell for a dog and herding and pulling instincts. This is quite a mixture, and it must be emphasised that individuals do differ; what one Samoyed does, another may not.

We'll give a personal example. All our Sams loved to welcome visitors to the house. Equally, when out on walks they developed a very keen awareness of human interest in them. Off the lead, most would wait until some passer-by murmured, 'Ah, look at... ' Then they would take off to greet them without waiting for any more to be said.

However, one we have at present, though equally welcoming to visitors in the house, walks sternly past anyone when walking off the lead. Indeed, friends wave at her as she passes them on the paths in our nearby woods, seemingly determined not to be interrupted in her exercise. If we stop to chat she comes back, walks off again, and comes back, demonstrating her impatience most successfully. Interestingly, she ignores everything else we see on walks: large numbers of pheasants, muntjac deer, badgers, rabbits, and other dogs. To her, a walk is a walk – no more, no less. Most of her kind would certainly chase most of these, partly out of curiosity, but mostly in response to innate hunting instincts.

You also may find your individual Samoyed will surprise you with unexpected characteristics during training. In Siberia the dogs were trained for similar activities from one generation to the next. We, however, expect them not only to act very differently but also to follow very varied pursuits. In addition to showing, some Samoyeds are used for sledging and agility in Britain. Elsewhere they also take part in herding competitions, flyball, weight pulling, obedience and as guide dogs for the blind. This demonstrates well their adaptability, though training for some of these activities requires considerable patience. However, there is no expectation that Samoyeds will reach the top in all pursuits.

BASIC TRAINING AND SOCIALISATION
House training

When you bring your new puppy home you will think only of very basic training matters. First and foremost will be the need for house training. Achieving this successfully and quickly goes hand-in-glove with feeding. At first, your puppy will be having four meals a day. It will also want periods of play, and periods of sleep. The important point to bear in mind is that after each of these activities the pup is likely to urinate, and to pass motions after food, though at first this may occur at other times as well. For this reason, you must make sure your pup is taken into the garden after every period. Wait with the pup to give it the chance to operate. Adopt this routine...

- early morning clear up – take your puppy outside
- give first meal – take your puppy outside
- allow it time for play – take your puppy outside
- let it sleep – as soon as it wakes, take your puppy outside
- second meal – repeat

... and so on with its four meals throughout the day. As you can appreciate, it is necessary for someone to be at home for the first fortnight when you take on a new puppy. If not it will take much longer to be clean.

When you first bring the puppy home it is facing being alone for the very first time. It has been used to a number of siblings and urine and motions have been cleared up quickly by dam and owner. Certainly you must expect quite a mess after the first night. Be patient, and don't show displeasure at this stage. Simply clear it up and put down fresh paper.

Fortunately, Samoyeds like to be clean so, if left in a room too long, it is most likely that your puppy will produce a puddle somewhere near the edge. When you leave your puppy for an hour or two, and especially overnight, place a reasonable amount of paper near the door you use to take it into the garden. Quite quickly you should find that whatever the pup produces goes on to the paper. It may take a few days to get the message, but the more you take your pup outside before it does anything inside the quicker it will be clean.

Naturally, the puppy will take longest to be clean at night, but bowels and bladder strengthen quickly, bitches being quicker than dogs. Once your puppy is content, used to a regular timetable of meals, playful activity and sleep, and not cold, it should soon sleep throughout the night. Then if you take it out as soon as it wakes up you should speed up the process of getting it clean. Remember, scent plays a significant part in this; dogs urinate where they smell urine. You want that to be outside, not indoors, so persevere with the newspaper in one place and ensure that, when you clean up, you swab underneath with bleach or cleaning fluid. If you allow the pup to play on the carpet, thoroughly wipe up any puddles immediately. The best way is to put an old towel down and stand on it, so that it acts like very absorbent blotting paper. Then use a disinfectant such as Cromesol.

Night-time noises

During the first night with you your pup will probably howl or yap because it is alone. How you react to this is very important to its training. A large cardboard box placed on its side and lined with plenty of old jumpers or Vet Bed should make the little one feel comfortable. Leave your puppy in a safe, moderately warm room of reasonable size but where it cannot get stuck underneath or behind furniture. On the first couple of occasions when it cries let it do so for a few minutes; then go in and gently reassure it by voice. Don't pick it up and cuddle it. When you have reappeared two or three times and assured yourself that your puppy has not got stuck anywhere, you must then harden your heart and resolve to stick out the next crying session. By now you should know what crying for attention sounds like so, if your puppy really is in trouble, you will know that the urgent screams are different. After a while the puppy will settle down, but the length of the process may tell you something about its character: laid-back-and-makes-the-best-of-the-situation, or determined-little-scamp-who-doesn't-give-in-easily!

If you give in easily and cuddle the pup when it cries, although it is perfectly safe, or take it into your bedroom, you are setting ground rules to which it will respond with alacrity. The puppy's on its own – it yells – you go and love it and take it with you. Guess who's undergone the training?

A laid-back character.

Lead training

When your puppy has finished its vaccination period, which, depending on where you live, your vet will probably advise is two weeks after the last injection, you will want to extend its normal play activity. To this end, your puppy must be trained to accept a lead.

First of all put a thin, rolled leather collar on your puppy. No other kind should ever be used on a Samoyed, or the hairs of the ruff will be damaged. Once this happens the outline takes a very long time to recover, if it ever does. Rolled collars are amazingly tough and bed down nicely. Let your Sam get thoroughly used to wearing one for a few days before you attach a lead to it.

Next, take your puppy into the garden and attach a light lead. If you hold this loosely, probably your puppy will show no great concern at first other than to scratch its neck. Then, when it starts to walk, go with it and ensure there is no pull on the lead. The puppy may stand still and give you a quizzical look. If so, be prepared with a titbit, which you hold in front of the little dog. Then when it moves towards the titbit, walk back a little to encourage your dog to follow a few steps while feeling the collar and loose lead. Perhaps your dog will decide to change tactics and run; if so, keep up with it with the lead loose. Then take the lead off, but leave the collar on.

Repeat the process the next day. By now your dog will have had some experience of the collar and realised that it cannot scratch it off. Provided that the collar is neither too loose nor too tight the puppy should come to no harm wearing it.

At some point in this routine, the pup will feel the lead tighten. It will then realise that it cannot go where it wants at that moment. Here again you'll learn something about its character: it may sit down and await events, or it may give an imitation of a bucking bronco. If it sits down, encourage it to walk by waving titbits; if it jumps around you must slacken the lead by going with it.

What you should try to achieve here is acceptance of the collar and lead as no great thing. Don't imagine your Sam's a young colt you have to break in. Samoyeds think their owners are the greatest things in the world. If you suddenly hurt your Sam you will damage that rapport to an extent. Your dog will get over it, but other training will not be quite as easy because you have now conditioned it to expect something rather unpleasant.

When you take your puppy for its first walk, bear in mind that you should keep its lead slack as much as possible. Your pup will meander all over the place, so it's best to do this initial lead training in an open space, not along a road. If the dog starts to pull you, especially if this is forwards, keep up with it and keep the lead fairly slack. Let the dog walk ahead and lead you. This is the ideal way to develop good movement.

As your dog grows you'll find this suits it very nicely and each day, after the first hundred metres or so, it will settle into a steady pace – steady for a Sam, that is. For you it will be quite brisk, but such a walk is far more interesting aerobic exercise than jigging around with a video in your VCR! Ideally, with an adult dog, you need a leather lead about two metres long. You'll find that for most of the walk you can have the end loop on a finger; the dog will walk directly ahead of you and, therefore, its legs will move directly forward and backwards. In our opinion you should always exercise a Samoyed in this way, with the lead in a direct line from the centre of its neck to the middle of your body. You'll also get plenty of practice in watching rear movement.

We strongly advise that you don't try to make your Sam walk to heel. Doing so does not come naturally to Samoyeds; if you want a dog to do this choose a breed for which it is a natural characteristic. For safety reasons and to be considerate there will be occasions when you hold your dog at your side on a short lead. However, if you try to keep your Samoyed

Perfect behaviour.

there most of the time on a walk you will get a very sore shoulder and the dog is most likely to pull away perpetually to the side, which will soon alter its front movement. You may see Sams who move one front leg out of direct line when walking in the show ring; it is usually the one on the side away from the handler. Incorrect walking exercise is the likely reason.

You will have to familiarise your puppy with traffic. Because vehicles speed past noisily and in great numbers it isn't easy to accomplish this gently. Our advice is to avoid making this your pup's first experience of the great outdoors. Later, when you go along a road the first time, position yourself so you are on the traffic side. Walk confidently yourself. If the puppy shies or cringes reassure it with a confident voice. Again, try to make it seem no great thing even if there is a lot of noise. Soon your Sam will realise that these objects zooming past are a part of life and, if the boss doesn't bother, why should it?

The distance you walk with a young puppy needs to be watched carefully. The growth of bones is complete by about twelve months of age, but much of that occurs in the first nine. Puppies start to 'go up on the leg' from about eight weeks, so for seven months the growth rate is rapid. During this time it is important that muscles are developed, but not overdone. A gradual increase in the length of walks, interspersed with free running, is vital. Just imagine you are dealing with a toddler to start with and finishing with a nine-year-old. This is a fair comparison between a child and a dog from two to twelve months of age.

Try, also, to discourage your dog from jumping up, putting its forepaws on your legs to get more fuss and attention. Doing this frequently doesn't help correct rear-end development. We know it comes naturally to many Sams, but in Siberia the human population was very sparse; here they get far more opportunity. From the beginning, when stroking your dog, bend down to its level. Then, when you stop, if your Sam attempts to jump up, bring your knee up to its chest. This will push it away. If this happens every time your dog will gradually stop, provided that it is stroked every time it goes back on all four paws.

Coming to your call

Getting your dog to come when you call its name is a most useful element in its training. It can be achieved quite successfully by exploiting a Samoyed's natural curiosity allied to its liking for biscuits. You can do this in the garden at first.

Take your Sam out but, before you let it run off, show it that you have a biscuit in your hand, break off a piece and give it to the dog. As you do this, say your dog's name as you would when calling it, but nothing else. When the dog eats it, praise and stroke your Sam. Then let it wander off.

After a short while, go close to your dog, let it see that you have a piece of biscuit, call its name again and give the biscuit to the dog even if you have to go right up to it to do so. When the dog eats it, praise and stroke the dog again.

Repeat this a couple more times, then try again the next day. When your Sam has wandered away, try to catch its eye from a distance, hold the biscuit where it can see it plainly and call your dog's name. If it doesn't come to you straight away, repeat the name. You may have to walk slowly towards your dog before it gets the message.

Keep doing this until your dog associates the sound of its name with the biscuit and praise. In our experience it won't take long before the dog runs to you every time. Then you need to try the routine outside in an open but contained space, just in case the dog's attention focuses on the distance at first. Persevere until the dog gets the message that when you call its name it gets a biscuit and praise out here as well as in the garden.

Then reduce the size of the biscuit. Quite soon your dog will come and be entirely satisfied with a few crumbs provided that it gets the praise and fuss. Very soon you'll find it will continue to come even if you only praise it. This should now be a conditioned reflex action for life.

TRAINING FOR THE SHOW RING

We are sure that many people reading this book will want to try showing their Samoyeds and we mention some aspects of preparing to enter the ring for the first time in chapter 10. If you want to do well your dog must perform adequately because, although it is in no sense a handling competition, the judge needs to look at your dog in detail for a short time. That's impossible if the dog is leaping all over the place. Not only that, it is highly embarrassing. We know because that is exactly what happened the first time one of us took a Sam into the ring. Needless to say she wasn't placed. We learnt quickly. Fortunately, so did our bitch – in the very next class she took first place!

Standing still

You will want to do this rather better, so start practising at home. Regularly put your dog on a lead in the garden and practise walking short distances, turning, and walking directly back again. Then stand still, holding the lead in your left hand and try to have your dog standing a little to your left and facing to your right. In your right hand hold a biscuit and try to get the dog to look at this. Hold it up, which should encourage the dog to lift its head, but don't overdo it so that it has to stare at the sky. Don't let the dog jump up towards your hand. The trick is to get it standing still for just a moment at first with its eye on the biscuit. Then praise your dog and give it the biscuit. Do this a couple more times with half a biscuit. The dog won't know the difference.

This routine needs repeating frequently. Change the walk to a triangle. Practise stopping abruptly; call your dog and flick the biscuit into its sight. Tossing it up slightly is a good idea, if you're sure you can catch it. All you need is to get your dog to follow your hand for a very short time, and then give it the reward – praise, then biscuit. Whatever you do, don't give it the biscuit if it barks for it. If you fall for that your dog will have successfully trained you!

Annecy's Turn Back The Time demonstrating the rewards of proper training.

Gradually lengthen the time your dog is standing watching your hand. Gradually increase the time before you let it have the biscuit – and gradually lessen that to a quarter. That way you avoid the danger of increasing its weight. At times make the same movement with your right hand even when you have no biscuit there but, when you stop, don't forget to praise your puppy.

A good time to add to this training is first thing in the morning when you let your dog out into the garden. Take a biscuit with you and, although your dog is not on the lead, toss it up and catch it where the dog can see. Soon you should find your dog will stand quite naturally and watch, hoping for the biscuit. When it does stand still for 10–15 seconds, praise it and give it the biscuit. It's an idea actually to toss the biscuit to the dog. Many a Sam will catch a biscuit thrown carefully in front of its face. This means your Sam has to stand still and watch you carefully, which is precisely what you want it to do in the ring when the judge is looking.

The Samoyed

It should be obvious that it is not a good idea to train a dog after a meal. Do so beforehand when it is beginning to anticipate food. Eventually you should be able to keep its attention avidly on the hand that is in your pocket or bag where you keep the biscuits. It may help if you have these in a thin plastic bag that rustles slightly to reinforce the anticipation. Although we refer to biscuits, we preferred using cooked liver when showing, using just a small amount. Although it is slightly greasy on the fingers it has a strong smell, which also attracts the dog's attention.

Practising correct show stance.

When you have your dog cooperating in standing still, try to achieve a position yourself where you can see its four feet. Ideally you want these to be positioned at the four corners of an imaginary rectangle. This is described most ungeometrically as 'four square'. Because this is the natural stance of a well-constructed dog, you want your Sam to take up this position in the ring, but think how often you stand with your weight more on one leg than the other. Dogs have four legs and so have more chances than we do to vary their stance. Look for this in the ring when dogs are just standing and waiting – there'll be plenty of examples. Once you know what your dog looks like from above when it is standing four square, you will learn the trick of gently pulling on the lead or moving your leg against it to bring it into that position without having to peer at its feet.

You must also train your dog to stand still while being examined by the judge. Ask friends to do this when you are training your dog in the garden, or when they come to your house. They don't have to know in detail about the canine skeleton; just get them to run their hands all over and look at the teeth. You want your dog to get the idea that this is no big thing and that humans do it quite often. However, you must try to avoid the dog associating this with a vet's examination when something painful happened. Normally, there is no likelihood of this. Early visits to the vet should be just for check-ups and vaccinations which, fortunately, Sams take in their stride. Anyway, visits to the vet are infrequent, so if you get many friends to examine your dog there should be no confusion in its mind between the two. Indeed it is more likely to regard your friends' examinations as fuss, so try to ensure it doesn't get excited.

Correct gait

Correct gait is important in the ring so you must train your dog to move at its best for the short distance available. So, while you practise those short up-and-back and triangle walks in the garden, watch carefully how the dog moves. It should move briskly in a straight line. Have it on your left and try to walk with the lead reasonably loose; this shouldn't be a problem if your dog is used to the procedure. At the end of the leg, pause and turn either fully round to come back or into the second leg of the triangle.

The main gaiting fault seen in the ring is pacing. Some dogs drop into this more easily than others. It occurs when both legs on one side are on the ground while the other two move. To do this the dog has to roll from one side to the other as it walks. Moreover, the legs on one side are parallel to one another as they move, whereas in the correct gait they move in 'opposite' directions. In other words, as the front left reaches forward the rear left drives backwards.

The best training for correct gait is brisk and regular walking. Then when you practise these short legs for the ring the dog should gait naturally. If you have a dog that paces you must learn how to get it to 'change step'. Actually, it's quite simple; while on the move you pull the lead directly upwards from the dog's neck. This lifts up its front momentarily and it has to change its lead leg, automatically correcting the faulty pace.

Ch Hilsar Silver Shadow sitting very patiently.

Ignoring distractions

The final training you need for the ring is to get your dog to go through its paces with other dogs nearby. It's asking much to train in isolation and then expect a dog to behave perfectly in the exciting surroundings of the ring with a number of other young hopefuls. The best way to achieve this is to have a party and insist your friends bring their dogs. Then take some time in the garden with them standing in a line while you put your youngster through his paces.

Not barking at shows

Some Samoyeds are unnecessarily noisy at shows but, in our experience, with a little care and thought you can train one to sit quietly on its bench or in its cage. If you arrive, plonk the dog on the bench and immediately disappear from sight to satisfy your curiosity about this great new activity, it's small wonder if your dog barks, because it's concerned at this strange new experience. If you go back, give it a quick hug and tell it everything's all right, then leave it again, it's obvious what the dog will do: it will bark again for more attention.

What is most likely to keep your dog calm is for you to sit with it first and share the new experience. Look around, and keep talking calmly to your dog. If you're nervous and excited you will transmit that to the dog. Equally, if you seem to be taking everything in your stride (you may need to be a good actor!) your dog will pick up that instead. Look for someone who seems well-organised and explain that you want to try training your dog to sit quietly on the bench, tell him or her its name, and say you'll try moving away but will keep watching. Then walk away to a spot where you can see your dog but it can't see you.

If it barks your new friend should turn to it, call its name and tell it everything's all right, without going towards it. Your dog is likely to respond to its name with curiosity. If it barks again let your friend speak again. If it barks a third time, go back into its line of sight but not right up to it and say firmly, 'No!'

You may have to repeat this, but your dog should begin to get the message that, although you disappear, you're not far away, that other people know its name, and that if it barks it doesn't get any particular satisfaction. That is very important. At the first show, if you can see your dog has been quiet, return fairly soon and give it some calm affection. Don't overdo it, or get excited. Later you can try moving away for slightly longer.

You shouldn't leave your dog alone for long periods until it has been to several shows. However, with caring practice, you should find it will contentedly accept benching or being left in its cage whenever and wherever you exhibit.

The reward

Time spent on ring training pays dividends because so often in puppy classes the one that shows the best is likely to win a high place. If yours is a very good example of the breed as well it is likely not only to get first place but to catch the eyes of the ringsiders as well as the judge. You may well see in the report, *This one has good potential; certainly one to watch for the future.* You'll find people certainly will do so! Then, later, when your dog hits the high spots, challenges for CCs, becomes Best of Breed and represents it in the Working Group ring, you'll be delighted you taught your Sam how to show well as a puppy.

AGILITY

As with all training, you achieve success in agility using the Samoyed's main characteristics. It loves to please humans and has intelligence with a sense of independence so, faced with an agility course, it may well see the obstacles differently from you. You expect it to complete each one in the intended way; in some situations it may see a 'more sensible' way of getting through. Furthermore, a Samoyed, as with so many activities, will run a course reasonably fast but with natural conservation of energy. It won't be the quickest compared to breeds with reputations for superb agility work. Therefore don't run Samoyeds in agility if you are highly

'Yippee!'
Photo: Sarah Styles

Hilsar Lethe doing just enough!
Photo: Khyger Studios

competitive or you'll be disappointed. Do it as they will – for fun.

Kennel Club rules state that training for agility cannot begin until the dog is 12 months of age and it cannot compete until 18 months. These are sensible protections for the growing bones of young dogs and were introduced after earlier training caused back problems for some youngsters.

You will need access to the obstacles used in competitions. You can make them at home but they must conform to the standard sizes and you have to ensure they are just as safe. The standard equipment is very expensive and items for a whole course will be well into four figures. By far the best way to undertake training is to join a club. Most require an initial assessment test for temperament, your degree of control and the rapport between you and your dog.

All training is done initially with the dog on a lead and a collar, which gives the best control. To start training for jumps, set one up just a few centimetres off the ground and, with your dog on the lead, jump it yourself to get its attention, then call its name and give the command, *Jump*. When it does so give it plenty of praise and a titbit. Do this a few times, then progress to getting your dog to do it while you pass to the side. Then progress to the dog sitting in front of the obstacle, still on the lead, while you move to the other side, call its name, say 'jump' and give it the titbit and much praise again when it does so. You then progress to doing the jump off the lead and gradually raising the height.

At about half a metre your sensible Sam will run underneath, as it can see what is now the quickest way from A to B! You must then go back to basics, lower the height, and put your dog back on the lead. Now it must get the message that 'jump' means 'over the top'. You also have to include the signal of raising your arm to the obstacle as you both run up to it and you say 'jump'. You also need to get your dog used to being either on your left or right. Each time your dog does things incorrectly you have to go back a step or two without getting annoyed or impatient; each time it does what you want you give plenty of praise and the occasional titbit.

**Father and daugher racing –
Dad's in front!**

Next, introduce a second obstacle, for example the dog walk. This is three planks, each about 3m long; the dog walks up one, along the second, which is over a metre off the ground, and down the third. At the top of the first and the bottom of the third is a yellow contact point which the dog's feet must touch; otherwise a five-point penalty is incurred in competition.

Again, training starts with the dog on lead and collar; the handler holds a titbit in front of the dog's nose and gives much verbal encouragement. Samoyeds, being fairly bold, are usually quite good at this, but after a time one can get blasé and miss the contact point at the end by jumping off. Training to a command of *Feet* at

The dog walk.

this point is useful to get the dog to stand at the bottom with its back feet in the required area; then the release command can be given.

The same basic training process is required for the other obstacles, typically the tyre, the weaving poles and the tunnel, though these involve actions that are somewhat more unusual for the dog. You can start with the tyre, using one from a local garage and setting it up on the floor. Sit the dog on one side, pass the lead through the tyre, get eye contact with the dog, call its name and command *Tyre through*. Give the usual reward when it does. Gradually raise the tyre from the floor, but block underneath it, or you know what your Sam will do! Later you'll get it to accept the competition tyre on a frame suspended from the four corners.

Getting your Sam to start going through the weaving poles may require two rows of mesh on either side high enough to prevent it jumping over, with poles so positioned that it cannot run down the central space without weaving between them. You put the dog at one end and call it to the other, waving a titbit. Later you can progress to the proper line of close poles and get your dog to weave in and out with a titbit held right in front of its nose.

It is probably best to do this under the aegis of a training club, as it is with the tunnel, which may need to be of the collapsible concertina type, so that the dog can see your face at the end when it begins learning to run through. As with the other obstacles, progression has to be gradual; the dog must learn clear signals and learn precisely what you mean by them.

No doubt you will get plenty of fun and amusement from working with a Sam in agility, provided that you approach it in that vein. However, if you want to excel, buy a Collie instead.

SLEDGING

More properly this is called *mushing*. Most Samoyeds pull naturally and some individuals are amazingly strong for their size. A few owners in Britain have taken up the sport and run teams regularly, and rather more do so abroad. There is no doubt that the sight of a Samoyed team racing across the snow with tails waving and tongues lolling is quite superb. However, if you are tempted to try it, remember that the breed's characteristic for expending energy over long periods is achieved by economy of effort. The result is a steady pace. Samoyeds will outlast the faster teams of other breeds, such as Siberian Huskies, but they won't beat them in time trials. Once again, it's a matter of doing it for fun if you decide to train a team of Samoyeds for sledge dog rallies.

Aviemore, January 1997: David Cox drives a strong team, all of whom were also show winners in 1997.
Photo: Peter Jolly

The training for this sport takes many months. If you are seriously interested you will be well advised to contact people who run Sam teams. There are clubs that hold rallies (they are not called races) largely during the winter and it may be a good idea to visit one or two events before you make up your mind. In addition to training a number of dogs you will need to purchase equipment: harnesses, lines, a rig, a sledge and protective items such as booties for the dogs. A rig is the three-wheeled vehicle the dogs pull instead of a sledge when there's no snow on the ground.

Wendy Drummond and six Sasoolka Samoyeds throughly enjoying a rally.
Photo: Paul Norris.

Probably the best place to see Samoyed teams in action in Britain is at Aviemore, Scotland, where an annual rally is held. Usually this has snow, though that cannot be guaranteed. It is pleasing to record that most Sams taking part in recent rallies also appear in the show ring. Indeed one such dog, the appropriately named Hurstbank Winter's Knight at Snowshe, was Best of Breed at Crufts in 1996 and achieved his champion title during the year in between his sledging activities.

A full description of training a team is beyond the scope of this brief survey; you can buy specialist books on the subject. You have to take the dog's natural inclination to pull and train it to run and pull with others and to learn commands. You have to develop a training programme that also gradually builds up its stamina. All this takes time, considerable effort and patience.

GUIDE DOGS

Samoyeds don't spring to mind under this description, but a few have successfully achieved the status in Denmark, where they are called *leader dogs*. To do so certainly taxes both the patience of the trainer and the intelligence of the dog because 28 words of command have to be learnt. Nevertheless, it says much for the adaptability of the breed that not only have eight Sams been trained recently for the work but the venture has been so successful that demand has outstripped supply. Once again, the foundation for training is a basic characteristic: Samoyeds love people, love to please and love to be regarded as one of the family. A leader dog experiences that in full measure because it goes everywhere with its human companion.

THE USA SCENE

Several competitive activities available for Samoyeds lead to official American Kennel Club titles. Nowadays, breed speciality shows often include such competitions, as does the annual National Specialty. At the 1996 Specialty, held in the Northwest, 245 Samoyeds competed in pack carrying, weight pulling, sheep herding or ran the agility course. This is excellent for the breed and certainly is re-establishing its working capabilities in a form suited to our fun-loving pet ownership.

There are 18 official titles, in addition to Champion (Conformation), for which an American Samoyed can compete. These cover obedience, utility, tracking, herding and agility. Titles are listed after a dog's name; some are amassing quite a collection, such as the following two 1996 competitors:

- White Wolf Wild & Free, CD, PT, WSX, CGC, TDI, JJHD-s
- Ch Hoof n'Paws Midknight Maxx, WDX, CGC, TDI, WS, HCT-s

More may soon be added. Furthermore, The Samoyed Club of America has instituted a Working Samoyed Honor Roll and accord the title *Working Samoyed (WS)* to any one which has earned at least 1000 points in one or a combination of these activities: sled racing, excursion sledding, weight pulling, packing, skijoring, therapy, and herding instinct.

SUMMARY

Successful training of Samoyeds requires:

- an understanding of the breed's characteristics
- assessing the individuality of your particular dog
- working in harmony with both parameters
- understanding the exercise from the dog's view (its reaction to the particular situation)
- patience and perseverance.

The intelligence and adaptability of the Samoyed will enable you to do much, but always remember that canine intelligence is very different from the human variety. Above all, whatever training you undertake should be enjoyable for both of you.

A Danish rescue bitch, Maggi, retrained as a leader dog. Pictured with blind owner, Merete.

CHAPTER SIX

Grooming

A well-groomed Samoyed is delightful. Its double white or cream coat, resplendent with silver tips sparkling in the sunlight, is beautiful wherever the dog may be: in a colourful garden, on a beach or on crystalline snow.

Of course, it can appear otherwise, especially so if little attention is paid to grooming. This isn't necessarily arduous but it does need to be regular. The dogs themselves don't like to be dirty for very long so, if they enjoy a walk in muddy conditions, you must expect to do some work to keep them in the condition they deserve.

Your new puppy should be groomed daily to familiarise it with the process; indeed, the breeder has probably started this. The act of putting it on your knee and gently brushing and combing it should be something it comes to enjoy and regard as a daily expression of the bond between you.

Grooming equipment for Samoyeds.

Equipment

Mason Pearson brushes, though somewhat expensive, last for years and do the correct job of penetrating and lifting the undercoat. The Slikker brush can be useful in removing dead hair or when grooming a neglected coat. Be careful not to overdo use of the Slikker, however, because too much hard brushing can break the outer hairs.

Combs are important because they do the essential work of getting right down to the skin and lifting the fur in rows. You need more than one. The first should have wide spaces between the teeth and is used for most of the grooming. You also need a comb with narrower spaces. This is necessary to attend to the baby-soft fur behind the ears, which often becomes matted, and the areas under the tummy and on the hocks. We prefer combs with bone handles to prevent soreness on the palms of our hands, but many people use flat steel combs without separate handles. Only experience of grooming will show you which type is easier for you.

Grooming tables are quite expensive but they make the lengthy work of grooming a Samoyed easier for your back. They have non-slip rubber surfaces which suit the dogs. These tables are portable so you can take one to shows, which means your dog has a familiar surface on which to sit and lie whilst being prepared. However, if you have only one dog you may feel this is an unnecessary extra. At home any table with a piece of carpet or a rubber mat serves just as well provided the dog feels safe and cannot slip.

Doing the job throroughly requires some cooperation from your Samoyed.

Routine

It is important that the process becomes pleasurable for both of you so that the dog is content and you enjoy the time you spend together. A dog that has been groomed regularly as a puppy will come willingly when you get out the brushes and combs.

Dogs like to be talked to when they are being groomed because this makes them aware they have all your attention. Never make grooming time a battle. If the dog becomes restless it's best to leave it and do more the next day. Daily brushing keeps the coat quite acceptably clean. The real grooming can be done once a week, when you spend more time and use the combs to part the fur and take out any dead hair. This keeps the coat looking fresh and the dog looking clean and spry.

When it is obvious that every time you use the brush you are getting quite significant amounts of hair clinging to it you will know the dog is ready to moult. A puppy will lose its 'baby' fluff and grow its true puppy coat by about six to seven months. This will then last until about twelve months, after which it will come into its first adult coat. Thereafter you can expect an annual shed, with occasional extra ones, depending on variables such as weather and central heating.

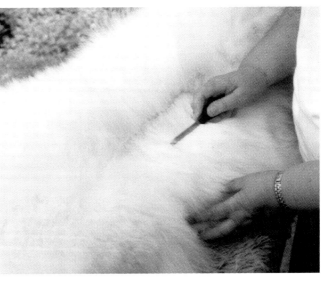

Part the hair in layers and comb...

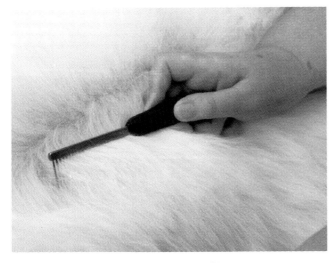

... right down to the skin.

Method

It's easiest by far to train your Sams to lie on their sides on the grooming table. They are comparatively large dogs and you won't want to keep reaching upwards to the spot you want to groom. Usually we begin by tackling the rear quarters because this is the most sensitive area, so it's best to get it over and done with. If the dog objects to its tail and back legs being groomed don't make the mistake of leaving them and moving on. If you do, this then sets out the real battle area when it becomes absolutely necessary to groom there!

One couple who had a puppy from us telephoned after some months to say they were quite unable to groom him. We went to investigate and it was obvious the hindquarters and tail had never been combed or even brushed since he left us. Now he was shedding at 13 months of age and was in dire need of grooming but, not unnaturally, wasn't going to submit to that without a considerable amount of negotiation! We finally succeeded and parted from him on tolerably good terms, but memories of the exercise prompt us to stress the importance of regular grooming of all parts both for your own and your dog's sake.

Always groom away from the body. If you hold the tail with one hand it can be groomed using the wide-toothed comb in the other. To prevent the hair being pulled, develop the knack of holding near the roots of the hair so the comb doesn't tug the hair at that point and any pulling occurs between your hands. You will find it easier to start at the base of the tail and then work gradually towards the tip, remembering to comb outwards.

Use the narrower-toothed comb to groom the lower back of the legs and the hocks, which are well feathered. Under the tummy, especially between the back legs, is a very tender part for both dogs and bitches, so be careful not to pull the hair here.

The body is probably the easiest part to deal with, although it is most of the dog. You can deal with it in layers, parting the fur in rows as you work up and along the body. If you hold the fur with one hand and comb with the other you will ensure the fur is not unpleasantly pulled. When one side is finished, get the dog to turn around and lie on that side and then repeat the process, working again from the lower to the upper part. If your dog is content to let you do so, groom the hair on the back of the front legs while it is lying down, especially the upper part at the 'elbow', which gets matted from frequent contact with the ground. Alternatively, do this area when the dog is sitting up.

You certainly need the dog sitting up when you deal with the front. Work from under the chin to just above the front legs, again doing a layer at a time. The narrow-toothed comb can be used for the hair on top of the head and behind the ears. Knots easily develop at the base of the ears and can form a hard lump that the comb cannot penetrate. Then the only answer is to use scissors and cut from under the knot straight along its length to the outer hairs. You may have to make two or three similar cuts, after which usually you can very gently tease out the knots. Never cut across the coat; if you do it will take a very long time to grow again.

When you have completed a thorough combing, follow up with a good brushing, always working towards the head. Never brush the coat downwards towards the tail because this flattens it. When you finish a grooming session, let the dog shake, and the coat will then fall into position and should be comfortable.

Many coat dressings on the market make grooming easier. They are fine and, having a deodorising effect, tend to make the dog smell sweet. Most come in spray canisters or bottles and are quite easy to use. Talcum powder is very useful as a spot cleaner when feet or featherings are dirty or the 'trousers' or 'skirt' soiled. Talcum also helps when the dog doesn't need a bath but needs sprucing up, and it will keep your dog sweet and clean.

Bear in mind that there are Kennel Club regulations prohibiting the addition of anything to the coat that can alter its texture. Nowadays, you can only use water on the dogs on the day of the show and there must be no residue from any other substance in the coat. For this reason, grooming preparations can only be used at home well before getting your dog ready for a show. There are spot checks on dogs at the show and any substance found in the coat could result in disqualification. No longer can chalk block or powder be used on a dog at a show, so your procedure must be to bath and then groom your dog without the use of any of these things for at least three days in advance.

Use grooming time to check for other things, such as cut pads or anything foreign between the toes. Grass seeds can enter between the toes and work up the legs under the skin, causing abscesses. Check over the body with your hands for any unusual lumps that may need veterinary attention.

Nails

Treat the trimming of nails as part of the grooming process. Well-exercised dogs with adequate road work do not usually need to have nails trimmed. The oldies, however, will need regular attention, as they are not so active. Nails grow fairly quickly and can cause the dog to limp and be in pain if not kept short.

Do the same thing using a brush on your Sam for final preparation at a show.

Nail clippers are readily available and simple to use, but you must be careful not to be too drastic when operating them. If you cut too much nail you will cut the quick, which will bleed profusely. Use the guard on the clippers to ensure that you take off just a small portion. If the dog has dew claws these also need trimming; otherwise they curl round and can go into the flesh of the leg. If you feel you cannot tackle nail clipping get a doggy friend to do it for you, or ask your vet to do so.

Eyes

Keep eyes clean of discharge with cotton wool, using a fresh piece for each eye to avoid spreading infection. Discharge stains on the fur can be removed with Diamond Eye or similar preparations. Eyes may be wet sometimes because of dust or tobacco smoke; if so, do dry them up with cotton wool, or staining is likely to occur.

Teeth

Get your puppy used to having its teeth looked at when quite young. If you don't check teeth regularly calculus (tartar) can build up; eventually the gums will become infected and there is an offensive smell whenever the dog opens its mouth. Regular use of dog toothpaste on a damp cloth soon familiarises a puppy with the process, and then a toothbrush can be introduced later. It is possible to buy a dental descaler to remove tartar but you must be careful not to catch the gums. If the build-up becomes considerable pet owners may prefer to let the vet remove it, although this is most likely to be done under anaesthetic.

Bathing

Samoyeds are relatively clean dogs and the normal pet needs a bath only every three or four months, depending on its environment. When the coat is ready to be shed it looks dull and lifeless but, when all the dead hair is groomed out, what appeared quite dirty can look surprisingly clean. Nevertheless, a bath makes the dog look and feel really clean and sweet. Bitches always moult after having puppies and appreciate a good bath when these have left. A show dog may need to be bathed more frequently, but this shouldn't be overdone because constant bathing makes the coat soft, making it lose the required harshness. For a show you

'A white dog?'
These pictures give you an idea of what Sammie puppies look like after a romp on a muddy day.

should bath at least three days beforehand to allow the natural oils to be restored to the coat.

Never bath unless you have combed out all dead hair; otherwise you'll have an unmanageable matt. The bath promotes the growth of the new coat.

The best place to bath the dog is in your own tub, using a hand-held shower attachment and making sure a rubber mat or towel is in the bottom to prevent your dog from slipping. Gather all you need, such as shampoo and towels, close by, as you'll regret leaving a wet dog in the bath because you've forgotten something. At the very least it will shake; more likely it will hop out and follow you obediently, trailing a fair imitation of a river wherever it goes! Remember to put cotton wool in your dog's ears to stop too much water from entering.

Samoyeds usually accept bathing quietly.

Many shampoos are available, but do not select one for a silky coat; this is not suitable for a Samoyed. Good green soap is just as effective as expensive shampoos. Wet the coat thoroughly all over with the shower attachment and then rub the shampoo or soap well into it. Rinse well and then repeat the process, using less shampoo the second time. The final rinse should be done carefully to ensure that no suds are left in the coat, because soap can cause skin problems and also leave the coat rather sticky. Don't let soap get into the eyes because dogs, like humans, find this irritating.

Squeeze out as much water as possible from the coat, gripping the hair (not the dog!). Then quickly cover the dog with large, warm towels; quickly because, if you don't, it will shake itself, giving you and the room a spectacular shower. Then lift the dog out on to more warm towels, wrap it up and rub well. Typically, a Samoyed becomes

'Do you think they'll insist on bathing us this time?'

quite animated at this stage of the process, so you'll have a large, wriggling mass to contend with. Remove the towels as soon as they are wet through and be ready with more. The dog will shake and drive more water to the outside of its coat, so rub it down well again until the excess water has gone. If it's convenient, let the dog run, or carry it, outside to shake rather than do this in the bathroom, but bring it back inside quickly, because the bathing has wet its coat right down to the roots and, consequently, to its skin. This is much more of a soaking than being out in the rain.

Hurstbank Troublelinsky demonstrating a really useful towelling bag.

To dry your Sam, use either your own hairdryer or the larger commercial type. Gradually move the dryer over the body while running your fingers through the coat to lift it and get the warmth through. Be careful not to get too near the skin because you want your dog to enjoy this and not be put off by being burnt. Don't start grooming until the coat is completely dry. Take care the dog doesn't lie about with a partly-wet coat.

Cleaning without bathing

If you want to freshen up a dog between shows, wet some towels in soapy water, wring them out and rub over the coat on the body, head and tail. Then wring out the towels in clean water and rub all over the dog again, doing this perhaps a couple of times to make sure there is no residue of soap. Each leg can be cleaned by standing it in a bowl of water and washing it fully, then rubbing it with a dry towel. Then the hair dryer can be used over the whole dog and the coat groomed when fully dry. This can be very effective because often only the outer hairs are dirty and this dirt is what the towels remove.

Bathing a Samoyed appears to be hard work but it need not be all that difficult. As you get older you may feel unable to cope by yourself. If so, get a friend to help you keep your pet fresh and clean. If such assistance is not available grooming parlours will bath and groom for you. However, if you do

The use of wet towels to clean off surface dirt is ideal when you are camping at summer shows.

Ch Novaskaya Xmas Star Lafay, spruced up and ready.

use one of these, make sure you tell them that Samoyeds do not require any trimming, not even feet! The exception to this is in the United States, where it is usual for feet and legs to be trimmed for the show ring. The service may be quite expensive but your beloved pet will appreciate it. No matter whether you or someone else does the grooming, you can feel proud when you exercise your Sam and people turn around to admire the beautiful white dog with the gleaming silver tips to its hair.

Spinning the combings

The work of grooming does provide a bonus, especially when a Samoyed thoroughly sheds its coat. The soft undercoat usually can be spun, depending on the staple (quality of the fibre), and the resulting balls of 'wool' knitted into very warm garments. Some people offer a spinning service and others enjoy knitting and occasionally produce items for sale on breed stalls at shows or for raffles.

'All right – time to take your coats off!'

Normally a Sam only sheds undercoat. This is fortunate if you want to spin because the harsher and longer hairs are unsuitable. It is also fortunate that, if your dog needs a bath at the same time as it sheds, you must comb out the undercoat first as described above, and this suits the spinner. It is very difficult to spin washed combings because the natural oils are missing; consequently many fibres become airborne. Usually it is the outer hairs of the dog that become dirty and so, when the loose undercoat is combed out, the resulting pile looks quite clean. Even if it doesn't, don't be tempted to wash the combings at this stage or they will be ruined completely. You'll reduce them to something like felt.

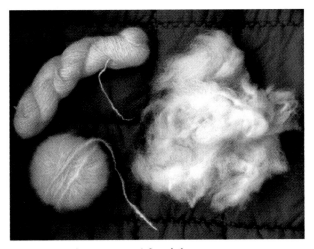

The raw material and the spun yarn.

When you have finished combing out the dog, remove any matted lumps, dirt, seeds and so on from the pile. Then simply put the combings into a plastic bag. They can be kept until the next shed to collect a reasonable amount for spinning if you have a one-dog production line.

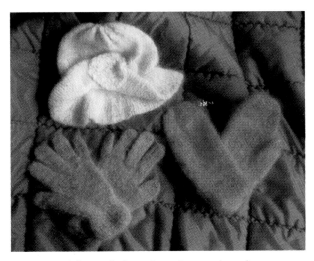

A hat and gloves from Samoyed wool, spun, dyed and knitted by Carol Walker.

Whoever turns the combings into neat balls of wool has quite an amount of work on hand, so be prepared to pay for the service if you don't do it yourself. The combings are carded, spun according to the kind of yarn required, plied, skeined, washed, carefully dried without stretching so that the garment won't shrink at its first wash, then balled. To this can be added dyeing if you don't want natural colouring.

Typical items made from two-ply wool are long waistcoats, mittens, cardigans, jackets, shawls and cot blankets. They are very warm, as you would expect and, provided that the spinning has been done well, very strong and long-lasting. Neatly lined and with well-chosen buttons they can be both attractive and a talking point. A lady's waistcoat requires about 0.9kg (2lb) wool; a cardigan about 1.1kg (2.5lb). A typical ball of wool of diameter 10–11.5cm (4–4.5in) weighs about 113g (4oz).

The interesting question is, how much do you get from your Samoyed when it decides to part with its undercoat? The answer varies between dogs and bitches and also according to the age of the dog, the density of coat and the extent of the shed. It has been known for one dog to provide enough for a cardigan at a single shed, but this is rare. Probably you will get around 0.45kg (1lb) at a springtime shed, which makes up into four balls of wool if most can be used. Two such sheds, or two dogs, might give you enough for a waistcoat, though three is the more likely optimum. Inevitably these figures are approximations.

Lucy Rhodes modelling garments made from Samoyed wool.

(Right) Jacket by Rose Lewis.

(Above) Jacket by Rose Lewis, hat and gloves are by Carol Walker.

CHAPTER **seven**

Health Matters

Normal Samoyeds in good health are interested in everything around them. Generally speaking, they are very healthy dogs with a fairly long life span, often living for 14–16 years. As with all breeds, however, there are times when things are not quite right. The first sign of a dog being off-colour is when it refuses food, or doesn't dance about with delight at the sight of its lead.

Correct feeding and attention to general hygiene around the home and wherever your dogs are kept helps to keep their environment relatively free from infection. Dogs, however, need regular exercise to keep their bodies in good condition. Most enjoy a romp in a nearby park or open space, which is when they like to investigate anything and everything. There is quite a possibility of an infection being passed to the dog during this entirely natural activity. The best protection is to keep your dog in good condition, enabling it to throw off infection more easily.

We are cautious about giving veterinary advice because we have no qualifications in this area. However, when you spend much of your life with

Samoyeds need to live active lives if they are to remain in top condition.

dogs and dog people you collect many interesting tips and items of knowledge about health matters. We also thank Dr Serena Brownlie-Sykes, a vet, for much of the following.

ALPHABETICAL LIST OF TERMS
Anal glands

If your dog starts to squat and rub its bottom on the ground this is usually due to impacted anal glands. There are two of these, one on each side of the anus, and they exude a very unpleasant and foul-smelling substance when the dog passes faeces. Today, because of changed feeding methods, there is often insufficient bulk in the diet, and this causes this problem. The glands become full and hard and the dog is unable to relieve them. You can learn to empty these glands yourself but it is not a pleasant task. If they are not relieved an abscess may form which, when it bursts, leads to an unpleasant wound and breakdown of the surrounding tissue. A visit to your veterinary surgeon once every three months for the glands to be emptied takes care of the problem.

Bloat

This is gastric torsion and occurs mostly in larger, deep-chested breeds of dog. The condition occurs when the stomach is full of fermenting food and gas. The stomach twists under pressure, blocking both the entrance from the throat and the exit to the small intestine. Inevitably the abdomen becomes very distended and feels very tight and drum-like. The dog may try to vomit or pass a motion but the twisting of the stomach means nothing can pass.

This is an extreme emergency. You must get your dog to a vet immediately so that he or she can release the gas and empty the contents of the stomach. The urgency is because your dog cannot endure such stress and the condition can be fatal in a short time.

The precise cause of the condition is unknown but common factors tend to be exercise after eating, lots of water on top of dry meals, and the stomach overloaded with one large meal. It has not happened frequently in Samoyeds but one male champion died from it. It is often wise to give a big dog two smaller meals a day and not to exercise it too near to feeding time or immediately after the main meal.

Canker

This is a rather old-fashioned term used for problems of the ear. If you see your dog continually shaking its head or holding the ears in an abnormal position it is best to seek veterinary advice. Constant scratching often means the dog has ear mites. You should never poke about in the dog's ears because it is fairly easy to go too far and damage the ear drum. We mention in chapter 6 that you should prevent water from entering the ears when bathing your dog, but ears should be kept clean and free from wax deposits.

The best way to clean the ears is, using a swab of cotton wool dipped in olive oil, to wipe gently and cleanse just inside where you can see the skin. Samoyed ears are usually well furred inside as a protection in the extreme climate of their native lands. Do not be tempted to cut this fur. If ear mites are present there will be a nasty brown discharge and quite an unpleasant smell, which you will notice when cleaning the upper part of the ear. There are many good veterinary preparations and your vet will usually give you drops such as Otodex to clear up the problem.

Ch Fairvilla Emerald in peak condition.

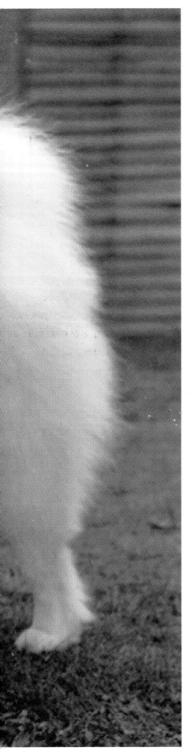

Cleft palate

This describes a failure of the bones in the roof of the mouth to fuse together properly. Puppies born with cleft palates cannot suck properly and so will probably die, or the veterinary surgeon will advise euthanasia. Several Samoyed litters have been born with this problem.

Condition

A healthy dog has a good coat of the correct texture. A bright, clear eye and a cold wet nose are also signs of good health, but not all Samoyeds have wet noses; some are drier than others. However, a healthy nose is never encrusted with discharge. The body condition depends to a certain extent on the type of life style it leads; obviously, a Samoyed used in sledge racing carries less weight than a family pet who goes for sedate walks in the local park.

It is important that dogs are not grossly over- or underweight. The ribs should not be so prominent that you would be able to see them were it not for the coat, but you should be able to feel them with your hands. Excess weight puts a strain on all parts of the body. Samoyeds tend to pile on weight across the shoulders if they are not sufficiently exercised.

Conjunctivitis

This is inflammation of the lining of the eyelid. There may be constant weeping or discharge from the eye. The dog may rub its head along the floor or against furniture to ease the irritation. It can be caused by very narrow or blocked tear ducts, ingrowing eyelashes or an infection. It should be dealt with by a vet, who will give you eye drops or ointment to put into the eye. This is quite easy to do; you should lift the upper lid gently and allow the drops to fall onto the eye. Do not touch the eye. Ointment is best put in by pulling the bottom eyelid slightly down and running the ointment along it.

It is important to keep the eyes clean if there is any discharge. This can be done using a piece of cotton wool dipped in slightly warm water and wiped round the eye. Never re-use a swab; always use a fresh one each time you wipe an eye, or you could transfer infection from one to the other.

Very recently the British Veterinary Association has found evidence of corneal lipidosis in Samoyeds and has put the breed on the list for observation. Basically, the condition is a fatty deposit on the cornea. Usually it is discovered during an eye examination or seen by the owners. It seems to be connected with diet so, if the condition is diagnosed, advice from your vet should help.

Coprophagy

Pet owners get very disturbed about this when it occurs. It is the very unpleasant habit some dogs have of eating their own faeces. If the dog is a pet in a family where there are several children, parents' concern is understandable. There doesn't seem to be a consensus of opinion about what causes the problem. It may be a habit the puppy started early on after its mother stopped clearing up. There is some suggestion that it is caused by insufficient stomach enzymes to digest carbohydrates, or a hormone imbalance. A deficiency of vitamin B has also been suggested, the remedy being yeast tablets or raw green vegetables. A deficiency of phosphorus is another suggestion, the remedy being to give plenty of bones, which contain this substance. If you do, ensure they are large marrow bones so that bits cannot break off and cause intestinal problems. You can give bone flour instead.

We have not had this problem with Samoyeds in our kennels but, if you do have a youngster who develops the habit, we suggest you get advice from your vet. Whatever the cause, clearing up excreta as soon as possible is the most effective solution, as well as being most important in maintaining healthy surroundings.

Diabetes

Diabetes mellitus certainly afflicts some Samoyeds, especially, but not exclusively, older ones. As with humans the condition is caused by decrease in the body's production of insulin but, whereas a human will suspect the onset quite early, in a dog these signs may go unnoticed. The further the condition progresses without treatment the greater the danger of collapse. Causes are various, such as an inflamed pancreas, infection and the treatment of other conditions with steroids, and some dogs are more prone than others because of stress, obesity and hereditary influences.

Typical signs are an increase in hunger and thirst accompanied by loss of weight, despite the extra food. There may also be resulting changes in normal behaviour, such as urinating in the house. Cataracts may form in the eyes leading to vision problems. The vet performs tests to check levels of glucose in the urine and the blood.

Owners can easily be trained by vets to give the necessary regular injections and the dog's diet and exercise routine has to be strictly controlled. Fortunately, as with humans, proper nursing works wonders and diabetic Samoyeds can and do live happy and contented lives.

Elimination

Male dogs normally urinate many times when walking because they are marking their territory. Young dogs don't lift a leg to urinate until they are between seven and nine months old; until then they squat like bitches. However, if a male who normally lifts his leg suddenly starts to squat, veterinary advice should be sought. Perhaps it seems odd to take an interest in urination, but this, along with checks on bowel motions, indicates much about your dog's health. Most pass bowel movements once or twice a day; these should be firm but not so hard that they cause the dog to strain, suggesting inadequate fluid.

Diarrhoea can be caused by something the dog has eaten and is the body's way of getting rid of an unacceptable substance. With a Samoyed the result can be messy, but it is not necessarily serious unless prolonged. If it doesn't clear up within 12 hours it must be treated urgently by a vet, because dogs can become dehydrated very quickly indeed. When diarrhoea first appears it is sensible to remove food from the dog for at least a day, but water, which is essential, must be available at all times. Going without food for a short period will do no harm. When the problem clears up, gradually feed again with light meals of, perhaps, boiled rice and chicken or fish.

Heart disease

Samoyeds do not suffer greatly from heart problems but heart murmurs do appear from time to time. Recently an eminent veterinary cardiologist who owns Samoyeds stressed that all puppies should be checked by a vet before they leave their breeder because any case of heart murmur can be picked up at this young age. If this is not done, the condition will probably be found when the puppy is taken to another vet for its vaccinations. It is the breeder who is responsible for making sure the puppies are clear before they leave home. If the condition is serious correct treatment can be sought. Some murmurs are of less consequence and the dog will lead a perfectly normal life.

Older dogs sometimes develop heart problems, but these are usually controlled by medication. Symptoms can be a dry cough, breathlessness and no desire for prolonged exercise.

Heat stroke

This is most likely to occur when dogs are left in cars or small kennels. On a sunny day the inside of a car can be like an oven and dogs die very quickly as the temperature soars. If you are at an outdoor event it is important that your animals are under the shade of a large sunshade or a golf umbrella, preferably where there is a breeze to keep them cooler. People who show Samoyeds in hotter countries equip themselves accordingly and the dogs are always shaded by camper awnings or large and efficient sunshades.

If the worst does happen it is imperative that you cool the dog quickly by any means possible: cold water bath, ice packs, a nearby stream or river – anything to bring its temperature down. However, don't lower it too much, because a low temperature can affect the brain mechanism. Even if the dog appears to have recovered, get it to the nearest vet as soon as possible.

When you go to shows or similar events in weather that may become very warm, make sure you have plenty of towels and cold water in plastic containers with ice cubes so that you have the means to cool a dog quickly. Never leave a dog in a car on a hot day, even with a window open. Many dogs die each year because of thoughtless owners.

Hip dysplasia

See main section about this at the end of the chapter.

Homeopathy

The word is derived from the Greek word homoios, which means 'like'. In other words, homeopathy means treating like with like. The use of vegetable, mineral and animal substances to effect cures for certain diseases was observed as far back as 450 BC by Hippocrates, the Greek founder of medicine. The present method of homeopathy was developed by a German doctor, Samuel Hahnemann, in the 18th century. He proved his work by using as a cure a substance which could also give malaria symptoms. The substances used in homeopathy are very diluted, and it was found that the more dilute they are the more effective they become.

There are varying degrees of strength; most people treat dogs with either 6c or 30c, the latter being more dilute (and therefore more potent) than 6c. The tablets can be bought from most chemists and health food shops over the counter; you don't need a prescription.

The remedies should be kept in a cool, dark place and not near any strong-smelling substances, or they become useless. Do not handle the tablets; shake one into the cap of the bottle. The tablets should not be given with a meal but can be crushed into a small amount of liquid or given in the middle of a titbit such as a piece of chicken.

Nosodes are made from disease products, such as discharge, and are used against the major viral diseases such as leptospirosis, distemper and parvovirus. These are the diseases against which dogs are usually vaccinated. However, some people are concerned about the rare side effects. Homeopathic nosodes can be given to puppies at a very early age. The natural immunity they get from their mother does not affect the use of homeopathic remedy against these diseases. Nosodes can also be made from substances such as grasses, house dust and soil as treatments for allergies.

Homeopathy is complex, so if you want to use this type of treatment, which can be effective, we suggest you go to a veterinary surgeon who practises it. More vets now use homeopathy alongside conventional medicine and are Members of the Faculty of Homeopathy. Details of vets near you who use this method of treatment can be obtained from Christopher Day MA, VetMB, MRCVS, VetFFHom, The Secretary, Homeopathic Surgeons, Chinham House, Stanford-in-the-Vale, Faringdon, Oxon SN7 8NQ.

Kennel cough

This is due to various viruses and bacteria in the air mainly during the summer months. The disease can be transmitted very easily from dog to dog by breathing in infected airborne particles, rather like human colds and flu. It is very contagious and if your dog has it you should not attend any dog shows or any gathering where dogs are likely to be present.

The sign is a frequent, harsh cough. If your dog does this you need veterinary advice at home; don't take your dog to the surgery because you could easily spread the infection. It is young puppies and very old dogs who are most upset by kennel cough, due to the possibility of secondary pneumonia. There is a vaccine which, when put into the nasal passages, gives protection for between six and nine months. We used this successfully when we went into areas where there had been outbreaks of the disease. Two dogs were given the vaccine, one quite elderly, and both were fine.

Licking

Some Samoyeds habitually lick their paws or legs and eventually saliva stains their white fur a reddish-brown colour which, especially if you are showing your dog, looks very unsightly. Plenty of preparations available on the stands at shows or in pet shops help to prevent your dog continually licking because they taste unpleasant. Bitter apple is one such product. If your Sam does this, check the legs and feet for any cuts or condition it may be trying to heal in its own way. Dogs' saliva is mildly antiseptic. However, Samoyeds are also known to do this out of sheer boredom which, if it is unrelieved, becomes a habit very difficult to stop.

**Ch Nikitta Winter Breeze, still in his prime at eight years.
In 1996 he won two CCs with BOB and RCC at Crufts.**

Old age

Fortunately, many Samoyeds live active elderly lives. We believe the best take some years to mature, reaching their prime at about five years of age and staying there until eleven or even twelve. The Veteran classes at breed championship shows bear testimony to Samoyeds' long-lasting capacities and quite often a senior citizen wins the CC.

Those who last to a good old age tend to be those from breeding lines with longevity as a characteristic who have been well fed, well exercised and lived happy and contented lives. Inevitably, however, the years take their toll. As your dear companion ages, do all you can to repay the fun and the active years he or she gave you.

Two small meals a day may be better than one large one. Vitamin supplements may be useful in maintaining condition. Exercise should become more leisurely: a lordly stroll to check familiar smells and give an avuncular wag of the tail to the newcomer down the road. Warmth is most important for stiffening joints and certainly a wet coat must be thoroughly dried if it rains during a walk.

More frequent health checks by your vet can minimise the risk of something developing unseen until it is too late. Check also for nodules on the skin or lumps beneath it, especially around a bitch's teats. Even if something proves to be cancerous, finding the growth early and having it removed may well extend the time you have together. Heart problems can be treated with medication and minimised with correct diet and exercise.

However, the time comes when quality of life deteriorates to the point when it is obvious your Samoyed is suffering, or has become weak to the point when it can no longer walk outside but has to be carried. If you have given your dog your best up to this point, as it undoubtedly will have given you – with the Samoyed nature it can do no less – you should consider euthanasia.

For our dogs today, this really is a matter of slipping into sleep because it is exactly the same as being given an anaesthetic for an operation. It is an overdose. We have cradled many heads in our hands as the injection is given. Though parting is heart-rending for us, the dog has no foreknowledge. You have to be a brilliant actor and pretend it's just another outing to prevent your dog from reacting anxiously to your feelings. If you cannot do this, let your vet take over. Euthanasia is the last kindness you can offer – when, in your judgement, the time is right.

Pills

Pills are frequently supplied by vets as the method of treatment for conditions. You have the task of administering these, which can be a problem, because some dogs are not particularly cooperative. You may try hiding one in its food and then later find a thoroughly clean plate with the tablet conspicuously isolated in the middle.

The direct approach is better. Open the dog's mouth with one hand on its jaw and the tablet in the other. Quickly get this to the back of its mouth by depressing the tongue, close the mouth and gently stroke the throat, thus forcing the dog to swallow.

This doesn't always work. Some dogs are adept at holding the tablets in their mouths and then quietly dropping them out at the side when you're not looking. To be sure, offer some water; if the dog opens its mouth to drink you can be fairly certain the tablet has gone down.

If the dog wins the first two rounds, don't have a regular tussle. Resort to crushing the tablet and mixing it as much as possible with the food your dog most adores; we find chicken and turkey rank highly. Failing this, try crushing it into milk and ensure it is dissolved as much as possible – otherwise your dog will drink the milk and leave the dregs.

'That tastes good – what is it?' Samoyeds love to explore new tastes, so need to be watched carefully outdoors.

Poisons

There are poisons wherever your dog is likely to go: in your garden, in your home, and on walks in fields, woods and towns. There are many potential dangers and slug bait and rat poison, such as Warfarin, in particular are easily found and eaten by dogs. In your garden chemical sprays, laburnum trees, yew trees and flower bulbs are all sources of poison. The list of things is almost endless, so try to train your dog not to touch things lying about either in the home or garden. Let it have its toys instead, which may include the slippers to which it took a fancy as a puppy and which, consequently, it favours.

On walks don't let your dog touch carcasses of rabbits or birds, which may have been used as bait for foxes. At home put everything out of reach of an

Always make sure that your houseplants are safe for curious young Samoyeds to taste.

inquisitive puppy or an older dog who can open cupboards. A puppy we bred died because the owners put slug bait on a cupboard shelf, but not out of reach once the door was opened. Recently a well-known Samoyed died after picking up an unidentified tube and swallowing it whilst on a walk in woods.

If you suspect your dog has been poisoned, get veterinary help immediately. If possible take the container or packet you suspect with you to help identification.

Pyometra

In this condition a large amount of fluid or pus accumulates in a bitch's womb. There are two kinds. An open pyometra occurs when much blood-stained pus drains from the vulva. This is reddish brown in colour and can be quite unpleasantly smelly. It can occur after a prolonged season. The closed pyometra is when the pus is retained in the uterus, often causing the lower abdomen to swell.

The condition usually occurs in older bitches. At one time it was thought to happen only with maiden bitches. However, this is not so: bitches who have had puppies can also become affected. One bitch we had, of another breed, had a pyometra at twelve years of age. We had the uterus removed surgically and, as we write, she is still with us at sixteen-and-a-half.

Signs are a prolonged season, excessive drinking, frequent urination, a raised temperature and abdominal pain. If you see any of these, do seek veterinary advice.

Scratching

When a dog has parasites, such as fleas, persistent scratching may be noticed, even to the extent of bare patches appearing where fur is removed. Most dogs scratch occasionally but, when it becomes more frequent, it must be investigated and appropriate advice and treatment obtained. We have been informed that some substances on sale for the control of fleas have harmed the skin of some Sams, so you would be well advised to obtain a safe preparation from your vet.

In addition to parasites, scratching can be an indicator of various skin conditions; for example eczema, which, if not treated, can result in loss of coat. This may then take a very long time to recover its full outline.

Seeds

Sometimes licking indicates a grass seed or something similar working its way between the pads of the foot. Some seeds are very prone to cause problems, especially in the summer if you take the dog for walks on agricultural land. Seeds lie on paths until they are dry and can easily be picked up between the pads; they can also get into a Samoyed's coat. Not only do they cause initial discomfort when they pierce the skin, but they can then travel up the legs or, if they have penetrated behind the soft tissue on the body, they can go anywhere. The danger is that an abscess can form, which has to be drained of pus by the vet lancing it when it is ready. By this stage the dog has had a miserable time.

Skin disease

Many skin diseases give rise to various problems, such as wet eczema causing loss of hair. The cause may be an allergy to something eaten, in which case a change of diet may help, though with today's variety of available food it may be difficult to pinpoint the problem. Other possible causes are plants, chemical sprays, reaction to grooming products, bacterial or fungal infections, and skin parasites. In fact, the field of possible irritants is very wide, so seek veterinary advice. It may be necessary to go to a skin specialist at one of the veterinary colleges, because some skin problems are difficult to diagnose.

Ch Zamoyski Lucky Claudia, an outstanding bitch.
This wonderful coat needs constant grooming to keep it in condition.

Temperature

Normal body temperature in dogs is 38.3°C (101.5°F). Two types of thermometers are available: mercury and digital. On no account should the family thermometer be used. Keep a separate one for animals.

The method is to smear a lubricant such as KY jelly over the bulb, lift the dog's tail and insert it into the rectum. The requisite time will be given in the manufacturer's instructions. Personally, we are not in favour of owners taking dogs' temperatures because a thermometer is easily broken in the rectum if the dog moves suddenly. Far better to have the owner holding the dog whilst a vet takes the temperature. You probably need the vet's diagnosis in any case.

Vaccinations

Most vets start to vaccinate puppies of about eight weeks against distemper, hepatitis, leptospirosis and parvovirus. Normally the course covers two weeks and a further two are needed for the treatment to give full protection. The starting age depends on the degree of risk in your particular area.

Vomiting

This can also be very distressing for the owner but for the dog it may simply be a way of getting rid of something it doesn't want. It may have chewed an object it found, or garden rubbish, and may then vomit or pass the offending item in the motions. Dogs should be discouraged from eating any foreign substance, but it isn't possible to watch them 24 hours a day, so these things do happen. Nevertheless, there is danger in eating things like packs of tissues, pieces of wood or bone, small balls and toys, because these can become impacted in the intestines, causing a blockage. An operation then is vital. Dogs also chew long juicy grass leaves, but this is not a deliberate attempt to make themselves sick as is commonly thought but because they like it. It can make them vomit, but this is of no consequence unless there is blood present; then veterinary attention is needed.

Nature's way of weaning puppies is for the bitch to regurgitate partially-digested food for them. Adult dogs sometimes do this and then eat the food again. There is nothing wrong if this happens occasionally, but persistent vomiting is not to be treated lightly and requires a visit to the vet, especially if blood is seen.

Von Willebrands disease

Recently there have been a few cases of this disease in Samoyeds. It is a bleeding disorder that is quite widespread in some other breeds. There are three categories, the third being the most severe. It can be inherited or acquired. Most commonly the clinical signs are bleeding from body surfaces that secrete mucous, which may be internal, and excessive bleeding after surgery or trauma, which also may be internal. In the inherited form both males and females are equally at risk.

It is important to be aware of the condition in case your dog needs surgery for any reason. There is a blood test but it is quite expensive.

HIP DYSPLASIA

The remainder of this chapter is devoted to a condition that is prevalent in the breed, as it is in a number of others. Over the years we have acquired a reasonable amount of non-specialist knowledge of the condition. By invitation one of us gave a paper at the 1976 Annual Congress of the British Veterinary Association entitled *Hip Dysplasia - the Breeder's Point of View.*

Background

The condition has been highlighted in the breed since the 1950s and no doubt has been present for much longer. In fact it is quite possible that none of the original imports had perfect hips. Any hip joint that is not perfectly formed is dysplastic to a degree. The problem facing vets and breeders alike is, how does anyone define perfection? Who is to lay down the requirements? There is no exact answer, but it would be good enough to say that the ideal hip is one that works very well, does not wear with age and does not develop disease such as arthritis.

The hip joint is basically a ball and socket. However, the ball is not completely enclosed in the socket; it is held there by powerful muscles which extend or tighten as the dog moves. For movement to be as free as possible the fit of the ball in the socket has to be very good and the linings of both free of any deleterious condition.

Obviously, the joint is three-dimensional. The problem of assessing the standard lies in the fact that the only way to see the joints in a living dog is to take an X-ray, which is two-dimensional. In an X-ray picture you look at varied shades of grey 'shadows' as well as the flat outline of the edge of the ball and the socket and from these try to interpret how well formed the whole joint is. Indeed, you look though part of the socket to see the ball. To read a hip X-ray photograph well you need to specialise in this part of the dog's anatomy.

When the condition first came to the notice of dog owners many vets took X-ray photographs and gave their own interpretations. However, although vets undertake the longest training of any profession in Britain, those in practice dealing with small animals owned by the public usually were, and are, general practitioners. The result was a very wide degree of interpretation. One vet would rate a particular hip very good, another would rate the same hip only average, and so on. It became obvious that X-ray plates needed to be interpreted by specialists.

In the 1970s The British Veterinary Association and The Kennel Club set up a joint scheme for reading plates and giving opinions. Guidelines were laid down for vets as to how to take the photographs, because a dog has to be positioned very precisely on its back and the legs turned equally so that the full edge outline of both the femur head (ball) and the acetabulum (socket) are seen fully. A registered number relating to the dog had to be included in the photograph. The plates were then sent to one of a panel of specialist scrutineers for a decision.

The scrutineer looked at a number of items to judge the soundness and health of the joints. Evidence of extra bone deposit showed nature trying to compensate for a problem, usually looseness of fit. Any lack of roundness in either the femur head or the acetabulum suggested other problems. But what was often regarded as the crucial element was a measure-ment of the effective depth of each joint. This was measured literally by pinpointing the centre of each femur head and drawing a line between them. Then a point at the upper edge of each acetabulum was pinpointed, lines were drawn from each femur head centre and the angles measured between these lines and right angles to the line between the two femur heads. The greater the angle the greater was the depth of the socket and, therefore, the better the hip.

This scheme ran for a number of years. In retrospect, we think it proved useful in helping breeders and owners gain some general understanding of the condition. This was very necessary because, when hip dysplasia was first diagnosed in some Samoyeds in the 1950s, there were varied reactions. Some people, not unnaturally, tried to advertise their stock as 'hip dysplasia free', imagining the condition to be like a disease – either present or absent. Others didn't want to know and so did not submit their dogs for X-ray. Some, on finding their dogs had good 'angle' scores, began to advertise a particular dog with, say, 20° hips (considered very good indeed) or 18° and 16° hips. This was a simple score that people could understand, though each scrutineer's report contained much more information.

In an attempt to help breeders and owners more, the BVA and The Kennel Club decided to issue 'clear certificates' to owners whose dogs had very good hips (in other words there was not much evidence of dysplasia) 'breeders' letters' to owners whose dogs had slight evidence of dysplasia, and 'fails' to all others. This meant that any one dog could be placed in one of only three categories. Furthermore, much depended on how good or bad a particular breed was as a whole in the matter of hip dysplasia. If the condition was prevalent then it was likely that few owners would get clear certificates or breeders' letters, which made many decide not to X-ray at all. In effect, what mattered was the average degree of dysplasia in any one breed, but to find that out the specialists needed many dogs to be X-rayed, and that was not happening.

The KC/BVA Scheme

In 1983 the scheme was changed to the current one of giving a score for each hip, which follows to an extent what organisations in other countries, such as the Orthopedic Foundation for Animals (OFA) in the United States, had done for some time. Nine items related to the joint are considered, a judgement is made as to the standard and a score recorded for each on a scale of 0–6 (0–5 in one case). A perfect hip would score 0 for everything, whilst the worst could score 53. An individual dog, therefore, can score between 0 and 106.

To match the two schemes the BVA and The Kennel Club indicated that the former clear certificate equated to a total score of 4 or less with not more than 3 on one hip, and the former breeders' letter equated to a score of between 5 and 8 with not more than 6 on one hip. A dog scoring a total over 8 on the new scheme would have failed previously.

Interpreting scores

Certainly the present scheme gives you considerable information about each hip and credits you with understanding and interpreting it sensibly. However, for the breed as a whole the danger lies in the very natural interpretation of comparative scores. Think back to school days. If you found you had scored 91.5% in an examination, surely you would have been very pleased? Relating that to the current scale for hip dysplasia that would represent a score of 9, which would be a fail on the previous scheme. The 'pass' mark (a score of 8) would equate to 92.5%, so you could be forgiven for thinking that a tough exam.

It's very natural to feel that scores of, say, 10 to 18 out of 106 can't be all that bad. However, there are other factors to consider. It is important to compare any individual score with the average for the breed, adding all Samoyed hip scores together and dividing by the number of dogs. That would be fine if most British Samoyeds had been X-rayed since 1983, but they haven't. Between 1983 and July 1996 only 775 Samoyeds were examined under the KC/BVA Scheme. Registrations during those 12 years were about 14,500, so only 5.3% were examined. This is rather a small proportion to project their average score to the breed as a whole, though there is no reason to suggest that, as far as hips are concerned, the dogs X-rayed were any different from the rest.

That average score is 12.8. You can see that this is well below what was regarded as the lowest 'pass' score of 8 in equating the previous and present schemes. So we have to admit that the available evidence suggests Samoyed hips could be better.

As a guideline, breeders can feel reasonably satisfied if dogs they breed score a total of less than 13, because this means that, as far as we can tell at present, such scores are average or above. Obviously the further away from 13 they are (towards 0) the better. Remember the phrase on your school reports, 'well above average'? A few of those, interspersed with some 'goods' and 'very goods', gave you a glow of satisfaction. Think the same of your Samoyeds' hips – that way we'll help to bring the average score down, to their advantage.

Hip development: heredity

How do dogs get good, not-so-good, or bad hips? When the problem first came into general view people tended to assume it was entirely a matter of heredity. Now we know that both heredity and nurture play a part, but no one can yet say positively what is the balance between these. Nor do we yet know the full picture of the mode of inheritance. Specialists think that total hip formation is inherited to some 25–45%. That is a wide band, but it does mean that 55–75% of the influence upon hip standard comes from the way puppies are looked after from the moment of birth up to the age of 12 months. Then they cease to be puppies for show classes and, conveniently, it is the earliest age at which they can be X-rayed, because by then the hip joints are sufficiently formed. So, in round terms, it seems that nurture has something like a two-point influence and nature a one-point influence on hip development. This is certainly different from the view we were led to accept years ago, when heredity seemed the dominating factor.

We were once advised by a specialist that, if four grandparents and both parents had clear hips (scored on the old scheme), the resulting litter would be 100% clear. We found this to be correct in one litter we bred and we were able to plan and follow completely. All four puppies got clear certificates. This suggested to us that heredity was paramount, but in retrospect both we and the subsequent owners may have also, and fortuitously, done the right things in nurturing the puppies.

The effects of heredity can be strengthened by line and close breeding. Therefore a mating programme using dogs with good hips eventually will improve hip quality, provided that the puppies are nurtured correctly as well. This, then, certainly should be the aim of breeders. The only way to know what is happening to your stock over time is to X-ray them all so that you know what you are dealing with and how your stock's hips are progressing. If a breed's average score is high, a programme of mating dogs whose hip scores are unknown is likely to result in the condition deteriorating.

Nevertheless, there are many other breed points to consider when deciding which two Samoyeds to mate when you want puppies. Normally, it would not be sensible to ignore everything and concentrate solely upon hips. However, this sensible viewpoint should not be used as a cover for not taking X-rays and not using dogs with low scores in the majority of matings.

Hip development: nurture

But what about nurture? What can be done to improve, or rather prevent damage to, the hips of puppies? Over the years various things have been put forward by breeders but, without controlled experiments, you cannot be absolutely sure which have the greatest effect. We can only give our opinion from experience.

In the nest the puppies should be put on a non-slip surface as soon as possible. When suckling they make treading movements with their front legs while the back ones slip and slide about if they and their mother are lying on a smooth surface such as newspaper. We know paper is very convenient as it can so easily be replaced when dirty. If you use anything else it has to be washed. Nevertheless, we believe this is important; the fact that the puppies' back legs have a surface to push on does seem to help hip formation. They are also steadier on their feet earlier when they start trying to walk and don't tumble and slide about uncontrollably as much as on a smooth surface.

We are also concerned about exercise in the early months. Of course puppies need exercise and they need to develop good muscle tone but, as with children, this needs to be increased gradually. It is certainly not a good idea to exercise a four- or five-month-old puppy by taking it on a five-mile walk at the weekend and then giving it no exercise during the week. Regular, but not overdone, exercise is the key to developing good movement, with the distance and length of time increased sensibly. Just imagine you are starting to train a child or very young teenager for distance running and how you would gradually build up stamina. In this way we are sure hip development is helped by the correct development of the associated muscles.

You should also be careful about the very natural tendency of a Samoyed puppy to chase about, darting all over the place and often tumbling over things. Garden rockeries seem to be much favoured. Add to this your own children, no doubt very excited about the lovely new addition to the family, and soon you can have quite a wild party. You must teach your children not to overdo the romping with a puppy, for immature muscles can be tweaked so easily.

One of the reasons for feeling that overdone exercise can be a problem in hip develop-

'**Exercise be blowed – I need my sleep!**'

ment comes from the fact that hip dysplasia does occur in humans and, indeed, in children. One aspect of treatment is to restrict movement very considerably to help the growth of bone. That would be intolerable treatment for a puppy, but it does suggest that too much exercise can damage the formation of hip bone.

There have been theories, and no doubt there will be others, about the effect of food and vitamins on hip development. However, this is as much part of whole body development. We doubt whether anything can be fed to a puppy solely for improving the hips, so we feel this is part of overall consideration of diet for a developing youngster. This is dealt with in chapter 4.

We have tried to give a balanced view of hip dysplasia as it affects Samoyeds. We were fortunate that most stock we bred had good hips, which means we happened to begin with good ones. One dog we owned (Sleigh Leader of Kobe) and used in the beginning of our breeding programme had hips rated as excellent. When he was X-rayed for another reason at 14 years of age his hips showed no deterioration compared with the plate taken many years earlier. He was an excellent and strong mover right into old age, and he lived to 15 years. We firmly believe that an active old age depends upon good hips and that we should do our absolute best to help our stock develop them.

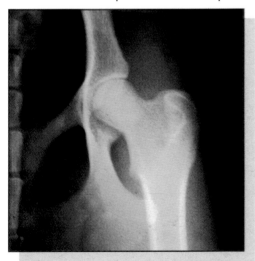

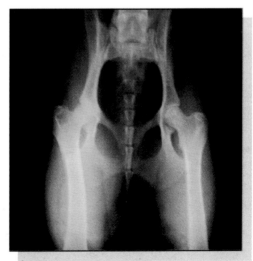

These excellent hips scored 0:0 under the KC/BVA scheme:
Annecy's Almost An Angel, born October 1995.

CHAPTER eight

Breeding

GENETICS

This section does not set out to be a technical introduction to genetics. Many books about the heredity of animals and plants carry excellent explanations, and we advise you to read those. Rather, we want to explain just two aspects of inheritance that every person who mates two Samoyeds, or two dogs of any breed, should consider carefully. Not to do so is, we believe, quite irresponsible.

Take, for example, a Samoyed with light-coloured eyes. This can be seen; it is quite obvious if the eyes are light brown or somewhat yellowish. Fortunately, it has no effect on the condition of the eyes but, since the Breed Standard calls for medium to dark brown eyes,

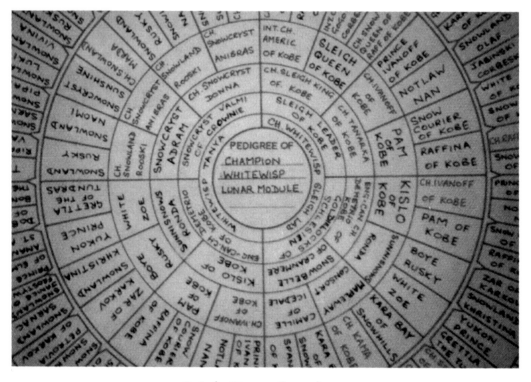

Part of a 10-generation pedigree
of Ch Whitewisp Lunar Module.

anything lighter is less acceptable in the show ring. If you have a Samoyed with light eyes but many other good breed points you may well decide it is worth using. However, you'll want to avoid passing on the eye colour problem, so it's natural to choose a mate with dark brown eyes, as well as all the other good points you're looking for. Then, when the puppies are born, you look very carefully indeed at the eyes, hoping they have inherited from their dark-eyed parent.

Ch Whitewisp Lunar Module, sire of 10 British champions.
Photo: Diane Pearce

The interesting fact is that most, if not all, of the puppies will have dark eyes, because dark brown is dominant, while light colouring is recessive. Many Samoyeds have both the dominant and the recessive forms of the gene controlling eye colour, but only a small number of puppies are born with light eyes – or, to be accurate, with eyes that become light brown as the puppy matures .

Every living cell in every organism has a nucleus within which chromosomes are located and on which genes lie. Chromosomes are paired, so there are two forms of every gene. Dogs have 39 chromosome pairs carrying tens of thousands of genes in each of the millions of cells making up their bodies. Genes controlling particular features in the organism are found in particular places on the chromosomes. Just one pair controls eye colour, though it is possible a pair may interact with others controlling other features. The resulting genetic 'pattern' making up a particular dog is exceptionally complex. In addition to everything you see in a dog based on the dominant genes there is an equally complex pattern beneath the surface based on the recessive forms of genes.

It follows that you must bear in mind that genetic influence can be both seen and hidden. What-you-see-is-what-you-get (WYSIWYG) happens with good word processing software, but remember that there are some programs where you don't see on-screen what you get in the printing. It is the same with inheritance. What is visibly inherited is known as the phenotype; what is invisibly inherited is known as the genotype. The forms of a gene controlling a partic-ular feature are known as alleles.

In our example, a Samoyed whose phenotype includes light eyes obviously also has a genotype for light eyes. However, all Samoyeds also have genotypes carrying potential for features that, although they themselves do not possess them, may be in their puppies' phenotypes. In other words, their puppies will show some of these features, depending on matings of particular dogs and bitches. For example, in chapter 7 we mention a few litters that have been born with cleft palate. If this is inherited, parents and other antecedents must have a genotype for the condition. Whole litters being affected suggests strongly that there is an inheritance factor.

Introductory books on genetics will certainly deal with Mendelian patterns of inheritance. This is the classic form first discovered by the monk, Gregor Mendel, who experimented with the inheritance of particular features of seeds and plants. He showed that, if organisms are mated that have either dominant or recessive forms of a gene or both, predictable patterns of inherited features are produced in the offspring based on arithmetical proportions. This knowledge is useful where the control of the feature by the gene is 'simple' (direct), and also where many offspring are produced. However, as mentioned above, some genes operate in more complex ways, and most dog litters contain puppies in single figures. For this reason, while it is interesting to look at tables of inheritance patterns for one, or two, dominant and recessive alleles in an organism such as a plant that produces thousands of seeds, it is rarely possible to relate that knowledge to inheritance of coat quality, hip standard, height, or the many other features you consider when you decide which dog to mate with which bitch.

Current research in humans and various animals enables us to predict far more accurately what offspring will inherit from particular parents. This involves mapping all genes in an organism. As you can imagine, it is an extremely complex task. Information about one such project in dogs appeared recently on the Internet: the Genome Project being undertaken in the United States of America, Great Britain and other centres world-wide. No doubt there are others; perhaps in the not-so-distant future we shall be able to view prospective matings of Samoyeds with considerably more knowledge than we have at present.

However, gene mapping at present deals with simple dominants and recessives. Polygenic control of features, in other words control by the interaction of a number of genes, is vastly more complex. So the ability to predict accurately every feature that parents will pass on to all their offspring is well beyond us for the foreseeable future. However, that certainly doesn't mean you have to mate them indiscriminately now – for instance, decide that the latest top-winning stud dog is 'perfect' for your bitch, never mind what's in his genotype!

Later in this chapter we suggest you look at your Samoyed's antecedents and ask what previous puppies were like. That is because you need to find out as much as you can about the genotype. You want to know something of the tendency for certain features to appear or develop. For example, in the matter of coat quality, you want to ensure that your stock has the correct, harsh, stand-off coat. This is genetically linked to biscuit colour. However, occasionally a breeding line with some biscuit in it will produce a totally white dog with a truly harsh coat. Such a dog obviously has biscuit in its genotype.

Over the years various people have tried to use such dogs to produce a line of harsh-coated brilliant whites, but gradually the harshness is replaced by softness and a 'floppier' coat texture as the genotype loses the potential for biscuit and harshness. In genetics this is referred to as lack of penetration of the controlling genes. Inevitably, to recoup coat quality, a breeder has to use another line with the desired trait to increase the penetration. It seems that Samoyed genes have a pattern in which coat quality and colour are interwoven. In other words, coat inheritance is polygenic.

The means whereby genetic make-up can be influenced by breeders is through patterns of breeding. Related dogs have greater similarities in their genotypes, so it follows that similarity is retained by mating relatives. Conversely, mating totally unrelated dogs produces greater variation and, therefore, a mixture of features in the resulting puppies as well as in what they pass on. Breeders recognise certain basic patterns of breeding that influence their stock.

Line breeding

This is the mating of a dog and a bitch who are related, but not too closely. The classic line breeding is a bitch mated with her grandfather, or a dog with his grandmother. The puppies receive enhanced genetic influence from what lies behind their parents because some of those dogs and bitches are behind both. Breeders often refer to this as 'doubling up', though that doesn't mean the influence is neatly multiplied by two!

With line breeding there is a tendency for traits to be emphasised. It strengthens the influence of dominant genes by increasing their penetration. Therefore, the good points of the parents and grandparents are likely to be passed on to the puppies – along with the bad points! It may also cause the results of recessive genes to appear more often than expected because these, too, increase their penetration, or are 'doubled up'.

Before you do this kind of mating be sure you have plenty of knowledge about the standard of dogs produced by the grandparents and great-grandparents. Make sure they produced many desirable traits and not many undesirable ones.

Well-thought-out line breeding can be very successful in Samoyeds in building up type: fairly similar dogs which, hopefully, conform well to the Breed Standard. This is what the early breeders had to do because they only had a small number of imports with which to work. It is why the influence of a particular dog, such as Antarctic Buck, was so dominant: his offspring were line bred to him.

Inbreeding or close breeding

This is the mating between a dog and bitch who are very closely related, such as a dog to its mother or aunt, a bitch to her father or uncle, or – closest of all – brother to sister. If you write out a closely-bred pedigree you'll see how often the same dogs and bitches appear behind the puppies' parents and you can begin to see how some traits that already stand out will be further emphasised. Occasionally, this can be an advantage, but all too often it causes unseen recessive genes to show their effects unexpectedly.

If close breeding was very successful in emphasising, or fixing, good points rather than bad, everyone would want to breed dogs this way. That most do not ought to prove that it is a risky business.

In our early years in the breed we bought a bitch resulting from a brother-to-sister mating. She had a really dense, plushy coat, super black pigment, and excellent movement. We found an unseen bonus later – her hips were exceptionally good, indicating that the hips of her parents and grandparents (she had only two, of course, not four) must have been very good. But she had a wrong tail set and something of a roach back. She was very loving indeed but was inclined to be shy in the show ring. You see the mixture? Used carefully, she helped to put desirable traits in our stock, especially good hips and quality coat.

There is no precise demarcation between line and close breeding.

Outcrossing

This is the mating between an unrelated dog and bitch. Most dogs and bitches behind each parent are different, so their genotypes are very varied. It is almost impossible to predict how these influences will combine and what dominant traits will appear. It certainly will be impossible to know what recessives are being carried by the resulting puppies.

The only guide you can have to such a mating is if the dog or bitch has been used two or three times before and produced similar traits with different mates. This would indicate that he or she has dominant genes for those traits. This is more often seen with males for the simple reason that a stud dog is likely to have more puppies to be seen and appraised. For this reason the belief sometimes arises that a dog can be more potent than a bitch. In fact, it can be true of either.

Outcrossing occurs to an extent because some people simply take a bitch to the latest outstanding champion to whom she may have no relationship. If he has dominant genes for a number of excellent breed points, this may be fine. It does happen, and in the history of the breed certain champions shine out for this reason, but such quality is rare. If it were more common there would be a large number of quite outstanding specimens. The fact is that champions do not necessarily pass on their outstanding qualities. It all depends on their genotypes.

Summary

You can understand why forms of line breeding are most likely to give the best results in Samoyeds when you consider their long-term existence in Siberia. They lived in great isolation with their nomadic owners. For this reason, most dogs belonging to a family would be related. However, when very close matings occurred, the resulting very good specimens would be kept and the poor ones killed, so the best would pass on their inheritance just as though natural selection were in operation.

The pedigrees shown on the following pages give examples of each of these breeding patterns. Ch Eastre was a bitch born in 1920, bred and owned by Miss J V Thomson-Glover. You can see that she had one paternal grandfather: the line behind Snow Cloud appears on both her father's and mother's side of the pedigree. This is an example of fairly close line breeding and you could say that influence really is 'doubled up'

**Ch Eastre,
owned by Miss Thomson-Glover.**

**Nansen, a son of two completely unrelated imports,
Musti and Whitey Petchora.**

because it appears at the same generation in the pedigree. The further back you look the more you see the same dogs and bitches repeated, which was inevitable because so few imports were available for breeding; in this case, eight. So you can see, for example, that since Snow Cloud's grandmothers, Kviklene and Pet, were sisters, his breeding also was quite close.

The matings of Musti and Whitey Petchora that produced

TWO EARLY CHAMPIONS

**On these two pages are the pedigrees of two early champions.
As you can see, the same dogs have a habit of recurring!**

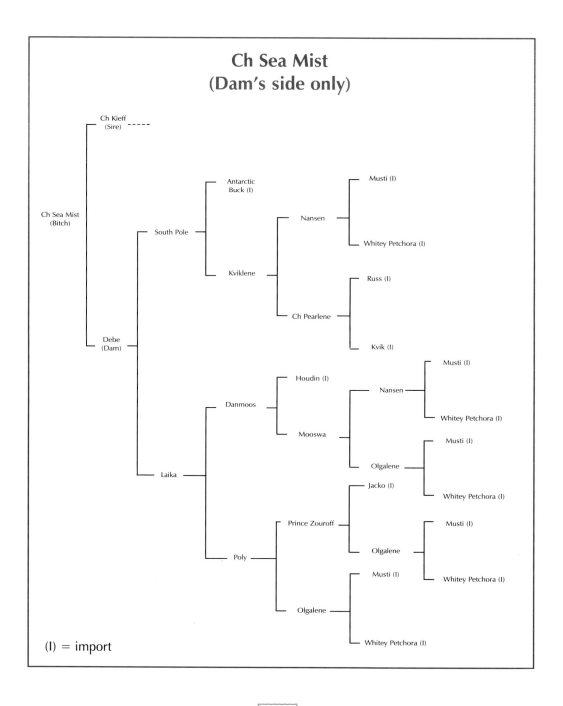

Ch Sea Mist
(Dam's side only)

(I) = import

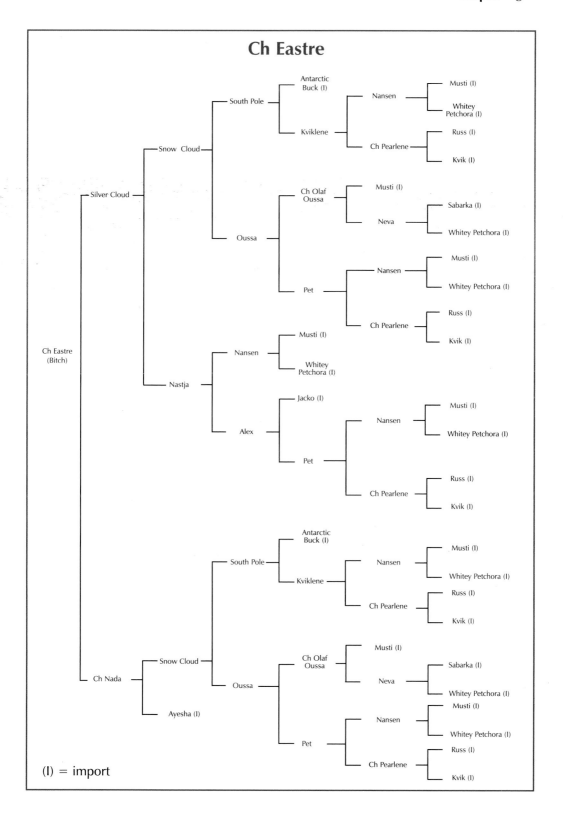

Ch Eastre

(I) = import

Nansen, and Russ and Kvik that produced Ch Pearlene, appear very frequently. These, of course, were complete outcrosses because the imports were unrelated. Nevertheless, only two bitches, Whitey Petchora and Kvik, were used until Ayesha arrived to provide a third line. Five males were used: Sabarka, Russ, Musti, Jacko and Antarctic Buck.

This pedigree reveals how line breeding, with some inbreeding, helped to 'fix' breed characteristics from what must have been the quite mixed genetic make-up of the originals. That it succeeded can be seen in Ch Eastre's well-known head study (page 109), which for many years was regarded as the definitive standard for expression.

The other pedigree is a section from another of Miss Thomson-Glover's champions, Ch Sea Mist, also born in 1920, and bred by Mr Hart. This shows the dogs behind her mother, Debe. You can see that Nansen and Olgalene were brother and sister. Because their parents were both imports, that mating would certainly have been a 'shot in the dark'. However, Prince Zouroff was mated to Olgalene, his mother. Thus there was considerable inbreeding behind Laika, though there was also a complete outcross to Houdin, another import, from the Abruzzi expedition. Ch Sea Mist's whole pedigree goes back to eight imports. It does not include Ayesha, so there are only two bitches: Kvik and Whitey Petchora. Five males are the same as in Eastre's pedigree, the sixth being Houdin.

Naturally there was considerable experimentation with the early litters and no doubt many fingers were crossed at times. Nowadays, we have more opportunity to plan matings with care and so preserve the wonderful features our Samoyeds possess: features put there over æons and developed by those few early dedicated breeders.

THE MATING GAME

When you own a dog or a bitch the suggestion of breeding from it will arise at some time. When you find yourself facing this, the sensible first question to ask is, 'Why do it at all?'

Increasingly vets suggest to owners of bitches that they should be spayed, irrespective of breed or whether they are mongrels. There is no one reason for this trend in their attitude apart from the obvious intention to reduce the number of puppies produced. Concern about unregulated puppy farms, the spread of inherited conditions and problems for the bitch in later life enter the equation. The old adage that one litter does a bitch good has very minor substance in fact, and one mating for a dog absolutely none at all.

If you keep a single Samoyed, dog or bitch, there is no reason why you should breed from it to keep it healthy. Its life will be centred on you and your family. It will see other dogs from time to time but if they don't come to live with you it is not likely that a normal Sam will show any signs of sexual urgency. Indeed, when the owner of a singleton bitch, two to three years of age, takes her to a stud dog for the first time, far from being delighted she may give an amazing display of non-cooperation. Similarly, a male presented with an attractive female for the first time may appear remarkably lacking in understanding. It follows that not breeding from your single Samoyed in no sense condemns it to a frustrated existence. If the situation in which the dog lives never includes sexual stimuli it will not suffer.

We sincerely hope, also, that you will not breed from your Sam simply to see what his or her puppies are like. All true lovers of the breed would urge you not to gamble in this way. We also hope you will never breed solely to make money. To do this with any hope of a reasonable return requires an extensive basic stock, large premises and a lifelong commitment to showing if your stock is to be sought after by people in the dog world. If not you will simply be farming puppies. Either way you will be taking on a huge amount of demanding work, day by day, with no respite. That is far, far removed from an enjoyable hobby.

Ch Sea Mist carrying her nine years lightly in 1930.

We hope that, if you are going to breed Samoyeds, you will respond to the intriguing challenge of trying to improve the breed in your small corner. That way lies considerable creative enjoyment, some ups and downs and a hobby that is on-going, bringing many friends and a very close relationship with these lovely animals. It will occupy a great deal of your time but won't take over your life. You'll still have time for a career or a business, although you'll travel quite a lot!

If you own a dog...

We'll assume you have a dog and are showing him. If he is doing reasonably well and is out of well-known stock, it is quite likely that someone will ask you to let him mate with his or her bitch. If he is your first Samoyed, and especially if he is your first dog, the natural reaction is to feel very pleased. You take it as a compliment, a further endorsement of his good qualities alongside those red cards.

We heartily support your feeling of pleasure – and heartily implore you to thank the enquirer and say you will think about it. Then go home and do just that.

You should then have quite spell of mental activity. Among the many questions you should consider are:

- For the dog's sake, do I want him to be used as a stud? Undoubtedly if he is used this once and produces puppies, which is most likely, and they are good, which is possible, you will be asked again... and again. If this happens, while remaining your loving and affectionate friend, nevertheless he will have a lively interest in all bitches, of whatever breed. If he gets the scent of one nearby you can expect him to go off his food for a few days and show every indication that he has something else on his mind.
- What do I know about the bitch? This question should give rise to some supplementaries:
  - a Will this mating be a form of line breeding, or an outcross; what ancestors lie behind the bitch and what do I know about them? (See GENETICS)
  - b Have I seen previous puppies from this bitch, and what were they like?
  - c Do I know anything of the bitch's health history?
  - d Have the bitch's hips been scored under the KC/BVA Scheme (see chapter 7) and, if so, how well do they compare with my dog's score?
- What is the arrangement to be between me and the owner of the bitch? Shall I ask for a stud fee now, or wait and see whether the bitch produces puppies?
- If she doesn't produce puppies shall I allow a free return mating?
- Shall I ask for a puppy instead of a stud fee? If so, am I going to sell it or keep it?
- If I keep it, shall I keep a dog or a bitch? If I keep a dog, I'm going to have a father and son in the house; if a bitch, I'm going to have a father and daughter.
- Should I write the arrangements down and get the bitch's owner to sign that he or she agrees that this is our arrangement?

Yes – there is much to think about. As you see, there's a mixture of considerations about the breed and about the arrangements. For most we can only ask you to think carefully as to what you decide. Towards your decisions we offer the following points. The first is what the agreed Code of Ethics (see Appendix A) drawn up by the four breed clubs has to say:

Stud dogs: Only entire dogs should be used at stud and not before 12 months of age. Members who own stud dogs should be aware of the need to improve the breed and enhance the reputation of the sires. They should refuse services to inferior specimens of the breed and to owners who have neither the time nor the facilities to rear litters.

This means that you are expected to make some enquiries. We urge you not to allow your dog to be used on a bitch without a hip score under the KC/BVA Scheme. Some people do advertise that their bitches have been X-rayed, but the greatest accuracy of interpretation of hip standard is achieved by using the best experts, and that means the scrutineers appointed for their knowledge by the British Veterinary Association. Then you must make up your mind what you consider comes into the category of 'an inferior specimen' in the matter of a hip score.

The matter of a bitch not producing puppies needs thinking about. If she has produced them when mated to another dog, but doesn't do so with yours, he may have a problem, but this certainly is not necessarily so. In fact, in our experience, it is rare for a male Samoyed not to produce puppies when mated to a number of bitches. It is much more likely that the optimum time in the bitch's season for the mating was missed. Remember it lasts for only about 48 hours in the three weeks, usually the 11th to the 13th days, though this can vary, even between seasons. However, if your dog has not yet been 'proved' by producing puppies and his first bitch does not whelp, it is fair and reasonable to arrange a free return mating.

Because there is such a short time slot for a successful mating during a bitch's season, it is quite usual for the dog to mate twice, usually with more than 24 hours but less than 48 hours between. That helps to give a time band for sperm to meet the released ova. Every bitch carries all her ova from birth; each season she releases a proportion, and that release occurs during the middle of her season when she should be most attractive to the dog.

You may feel it's going a bit over the top to suggest writing down the arrangements you decide with the owner of the bitch, especially so if you have become quite friendly with him or her. However, in the dog world, as elsewhere, friendships change. Unfortunately, when they do, attitudes may change as well. In such an eventuality a written agreement is a sensible protection against mistrust. Hopefully, you can put the paper away and it will never see the light of day again.

What to charge as a stud fee you will have to decide. Talking to other stud dog owners may give you some idea of the current range. At first you should charge the lower end; if, later, your dog wins well in the ring, even becomes a champion, you can increase the fee. In times past the average stud fee was about the same as the price of a puppy; today the latter has outstripped the former, so bitch owners are less inclined to pay with a puppy. On the other hand, the owner of a bitch who wants a particular stud's line can circumvent an exorbitant fee by choosing a lesser known, possibly unshown, brother. He won't be a clone but his genetic background will be identical.

If you own a bitch...

Some of the considerations we have mentioned above also apply if your first Samoyed is a bitch and you think about breeding from her, and several different ones will arise.

You will face all the work involved in whelping, rearing and selling the puppies. There is much to enjoy but much to do that is highly time consuming, involving not only considerable activity but also considerable inactivity while you endlessly watch your new charges gambolling and playing. Household routine tends to disappear for a couple of months.

Before you make the decision to breed, do have your bitch's hips X-rayed and scored under the KC/BVA Scheme for hip dysplasia. Then, be sure you know what the score means (see chapter 7). Having bred stock with a reputation for good hips under the Scheme when clear certificates and breeders' letters were issued, we would not be inclined to consider breeding with a bitch with hips whose scores were over the current average of all examined, which is 12.8 at the time of writing. Preferably we would use one with a total score of 8 or less, 8 being the equivalent limit to receive the former breeders' letter stating that the dog showed evidence of dysplasia but to a limited degree and advising careful breeding to dogs with better hips. We recognise that to set 8 as the maximum limit to consider for breeding today would be very difficult because there are so few with scores of less, so we would also consider a bitch with 9, 10, 11 or 12 if she had many of the other important breed qualities. We would be very hesitant to use a bitch with higher scores. The same thoughts apply to the stud dog.

The next consideration is which stud dog to use. This entails thinking about patterns of breeding and, preferably, finding one which will give you a form of line breeding (see page 107). We know there will be a great temptation simply to by-pass all the hassle of choosing a stud and go for the latest and best champion: the Best of Breed at Crufts last year, the Working Group winner at a championship show, or even that rarity the Best In Show at an all-breed championship show. This is most understandable and attractive. Surely if judges put up this particular Samoyed dog to the heights he must be good? Look what you can put on the puppies' pedigrees! Look at the extra you can put on their prices!

To do this without checking the dog's antecedents is to invite unseen troubles (page 106). These days buyers of your puppies have the law heavily on their side if you sell any that prove to have an inherited health or conformation problem. In law you are supposed to know about these things. Ignorance can be costly because you may be liable not only to refund the purchase price but also vets' bills and other financial considerations. Do be careful before you join the bandwagon rolling to a famous stud's door. The fact that he is famous should mean there are plenty of his puppies about, which can be checked, and you would be expected to do so. Enquire, also, whether there have been problems.

We'll assume that you choose the stud dog with as much care and thought as you can. Then you must decide at which season to try to have your bitch mated for the first time. Samoyeds have fairly regular six-monthly seasons. The bitch has her first at six to nine months or thereabouts, so her second will be at twelve to fifteen months and her third just after two years or so. In the matter of advice about which season to choose to let your bitch have puppies we stress what is contained in the agreed Code of Ethics (see Appendix A) drawn up by the four breed clubs, under the headings Breeding Age and Welfare of the Bitch. This speaks for itself and no loving owner will want to depart from it.

Mating

Having made your decision, chosen the stud dog and made written arrangements with the owner regarding the mating, you then hope your bitch will follow the rules. This means that she will give you clear evidence of the first day of her season so that you can calculate the eleventh for the first attempt at a mating. The evidence of the season (oestrus) is a trickle of blood from the vagina and an enlarged vulva. However, some bitches keep themselves very clean, and some have a very small discharge at first, especially young ones. For this reason you need to be vigilant around the time you expect the season to begin. If she hasn't read the rules she may keep you guessing for weeks.

If either dog or bitch is mating for the first time you need to be ready to assist, reassure, or both. It is better if one of them is experienced; a bitch who has been mated before is more likely to put up with strange antics on the part of the dog, who is responding to his hormones for the first time and may not even know which end of the bitch he should be addressing.

If the dog is the experienced partner the bitch will need reassurance from her owner, provided he or she can be calm and level-headed. We would ask the owner to hold the bitch's head, both for reassurance and to prevent her turning on the dog when he penetrates which, of course, will be a hitherto unknown experience for her. If she decides to resist nature by collapsing her back legs, a remarkably successful method of defence, you may need an experienced person holding her rear end and possibly helping the dog as well. With a long-coated breed such as the Samoyed, novice dogs experience difficulty hitting the target. The owner of the dog is the best person to do this but, if you are supervising for the first time, do arrange for an experienced friend to help you. Then, once your dog realises you are there to help him achieve much pleasure, he will let you handle any difficult bitches who later come his way.

You may have thought that mating merely entails putting a dog and bitch together in a small yard and letting them get on with matters. This has been known to work occasionally, but the potential for one or the other to be put off for good is so high that we certainly don't advise such a practice. We have learnt by experience that, if either dog or bitch decides not to mate, various methods can be brought into play to avoid that end, from total diffidence to never-seen-before snarling animosity allied to amazing strength. Certainly you should allow time for the partners to get acquainted. After all, it should be a natural event. However, natural cavorting about and general skittishness can escalate into far more boisterous behaviour, which is when instinctive messages can get confused and something very much like a fight ensues. What you want to see, after some mischievous larking about and sniffing of the genital regions, is the bitch standing and holding her tail distinctively to one side. At this point she should have a 'come hither' look in her eye and should allow the dog to mount.

Being with the dog and bitch at the moment of penetration not only helps to avoid the bitch snapping at the dog's nose, which will be in the vicinity of her ear, but also enables the person at the working end to hold both together briefly to assist the tie. This occurs when two glands, one on each side of the dog's penis, swell. Muscles near the end of the bitch's vagina then clamp over these and both are securely tied together. Quite soon after this has occurred the dog lets his front slip off the bitch's back. He may pause there, though if he is experienced he is more likely to continue to move his front away and swing one of his back legs over the bitch's back, finishing standing facing the opposite direction. There they will stay until the tie ends, which occurs when the bitch's vaginal muscles relax and she releases the dog.

With Samoyeds you may wonder what happens to the bitch's tail when the dog turns in this way. She demonstrated her readiness for the dog to mount her in the first place by swinging it well to the side. That's where it tends to stay, and experienced handlers can help extricate it so that both tails are more or less in their usual positions during the tie.

All you need to do during the tie is ensure that neither dog nor bitch decide to wander about. It is not at all easy for the tie to break before normal release, but if it does so both are most likely to experience pain. That is a sure way of dissuading them from wanting to repeat the experience and thus rendering them uncooperative in the future. Usually, both are quite patient. We have known a dog who would attempt to doze off, putting his forelegs on the ground and resting his head on them whilst the other end remained in place. A bitch is usually content to rest her head on her owner's lap, which she will soak with saliva, because drooling is a feature of a successful tie. Be prepared with a towel.

You cannot predict how long the tie will last and if you're the one on your knees officiating at the rear end it can seem ages. Anything from 5 to 45 minutes is likely; just hope you'll be favoured with no more than the average of 15. However, the length of the tie has virtually no bearing on the resulting number of puppies. Indeed, litters are entirely possible with no tie at all. What matters is how many sperm reach the ova in the uterus and, since there are millions, that can be achieved with a remarkably small amount of semen in the right place at the right moment. In general, however, a tie is a sign that the mating has occurred at the optimum time in the bitch's season. For that reason breeders prefer it to occur.

When the bitch releases the dog he may be unable to move at first because his penis will be extended. He will need some moments to relax, during which it will return to its sheath and then he'll be able to walk normally again. The bitch, however, may be quite lively and ready to prance about. It's sensible not to let her jump up because semen may well flow out of her vagina, although, hopefully, sufficient will have been deposited where this is impossible. Whether there has been a tie or not, if either dog or bitch is a maiden and the first mating was obviously an enjoyable experience for it, a second mating within 48 hours is a good idea to cement the feeling for future occasions. Probably this is especially so for the dog, who may get more of the idea on the second occasion. Quick reinforcement is better than waiting months, perhaps, for another bitch to come his way.

Immediately after the mating both dog and bitch should be offered water but not food. The bitch should then be put somewhere quiet, which may well be her owner's car in readiness for the return journey. Ideally, she should have half hour at least before this takes place. You'll probably need a cup of tea yourself.

PREGNANCY

For some weeks afterwards the bitch will continue life as normal and you may wonder whether the whole thing was a complete delusion. This again is nature; imagine pregnant bitches in Siberia, where they would have to live and work as usual. Understandably, though, you will want the pregnancy to have rather less uncertainty and more health and veterinary care.

Opinions vary as to when you can first tell whether a bitch is in whelp. Knowing your own well may help you to spot minor things long before you can feel actual puppies in the bitch's womb. By about five weeks after the mating this may be possible and soon after that the bitch may show signs of wanting more food. This can be increased gradually during the last two to three weeks; earlier than that is probably unnecessary and may cause her to put on extra weight in addition to the puppies. She should certainly maintain regular exercise so that all her muscles are working well and she is in fine bodily tone. During the last three weeks vitamin supplements can be useful. Do get advice from and a general check-up by your vet in the sixth week of pregnancy because he or she is in the best position to advise precisely about your bitch. It is false economy to skip that consultation and then find you have to pay for far more treatment later. You should also ask for and give her some worming medication.

If you have mated the bitch you will hope she doesn't fool you with a false pregnancy. This occurs when her instincts supply the wrong message; she acts as though she is having puppies, but isn't. It can happen even when the bitch has not been mated. Nine weeks after the middle of her season you begin wondering whether she got together with the dog next door when you weren't looking. A bitch can even produce a convincing swelling of the tummy, though she might be helped in this if you've been giving her extra food. She may make a bed, dig under the garden shed, start tearing up paper in the whelping box you've made – all to no avail. A day or two later she forgets it all and wonders what you're fussing about. Some bitches seem more inclined to this behaviour than others. It is quite harmless. What she can't fool is a vet with an X-ray machine or, better still, ultrasound equipment.

With your vet's help you should know whether your bitch has puppies. Near the predicted whelping time she will look for a place to have them. Usually, a bitch goes along with whatever her owner provides but she may show a passing desire for somewhere of her own choosing. Nature decreed bitches had to dig holes a few thousand years ago and it's remarkably persistent: hence the garden shed excavation, or her interest in the highly inconvenient low dark cupboard she can crawl into but you can't.

We suggest a whelping box about 120cm x 90cm x 75cm (4ft x 3ft x 2.5ft), with a top that is about 60cm (2ft) from front to back. This retains her feeling of security but allows you better access. You can increase her feeling of being under an overhang by temporarily draping a blanket over the extra space. Wooden construction is best, and you may wish to make one you can dismantle and keep for future litters, or you may buy a proprietary one. The front need be no higher than 25cm (9in) high and will need to be removed later. The bitch can step over this easily but very young puppies cannot. Inside the most important extra is a crush barrier. This is a firm strip about 15cm (6in) off the floor and away from the walls. The bitch will lie against this but the space behind prevents puppies being squashed or suffocated.

A crucial point is that the temperature at floor level should be at least 27°C (80°F) during the whelping. Why this is so necessary will become apparent when birth begins.

The bitch needs some days to get used to the box and to associate it with her developing internal feelings. As her time nears she will tear up useful material, putting her paws on it, gripping it with her mouth and pulling upwards with some strength. If she finds a supply of old curtains and sheets handy in this new piece of furniture she'll appreciate the gesture and tear some of them up for her whelping bed. Whilst in the box and doing so she may well decide this is as good a place as any.

BIRTH

The gestation period lasts 63 days (see Whelping Chart at Appendix B). You should keep a close watch on your bitch from the 59th day because some Samoyeds tend to whelp slightly early. Vets may point out this hasn't been researched accurately so we mention it only from our experience and the record of our litters. Looking at our first 17 Samoyed litters, which involved 9 bitches, 14 normal whelpings were on days 60, 60, 59, 62, 60, 63, 61, 63, 60, 63, 62, 60, 62, 63. The remaining three involved two caesarian sections and one with just one stillborn puppy. When two services were given we counted from the first. We watched very carefully indeed for the first sign of oestrus in each case.

Usually the bitch refuses food near the time of whelping. She may make her bed even more vigorously and appear somewhat agitated and unable to settle. This may continue for some time, up to 24 hours, or it may be much shorter. It depends on variables such as the size of the litter, how the puppies are lying, whether this is a first litter, the age of the bitch and, certainly, her physical condition. Bitches in firm condition and good bloom from proper feeding and exercise usually whelp easily with fewer problems.

After some time she will lie down and pant quite strongly for short periods. Later on these become interspersed with short periods when she goes still and may stretch slightly. This is when a puppy starts to move into the birth canal. Then she will pant again.

When she settles into a routine of panting, then stopping and straining, you can be sure a puppy is ready to be born. Hopefully this occurs without much difficulty and, after two or three obviously larger contractions, water is expelled from the birth passage and, shortly afterwards, a puppy appears in its membrane bag with the umbilical cord attached. The next normal event is for the bitch to seize the bag in her mouth, tear it and eat it, severing the cord as well, and giving the puppy a thorough and vigorous licking. For its part the puppy should begin commenting loudly on this treatment and decide that if this how the new world is going to treat it, getting a drink might be a sensible idea. It will then head off, arms and legs flailing, towards the milk bar.

Finding a teat amongst all that fur can be a problem, despite the fact that the bitch sheds some from that region as the whelping time approaches. Once there the puppy may make a number of charges at the thing without quite getting the message that it has to open its mouth. You may need to help by gently squeezing at the sides of its jaw with your thumb and first finger of one hand, gently squeezing behind the teat with the same fingers of the other hand to produce a few spots of milk. Then, when the pup opens its mouth you bring the two together and lock-on is achieved.

Sometimes the birth is fine and the pup arrives in its bag, but the bitch seems rather unconcerned as to what has happened. In this case you must tear the bag quickly, putting a finger under the puppy's chin and pulling the bag away, put the pup on a towel in your hand

and start rubbing its back quite strongly towards the head which should be sloping downwards to help mucous drain away from the nose. Do this close to your bitch's face, encouraging her while trying to make the puppy take its first breath and squeak. Your bitch should find this quite curious and then, when it cries, maternal instincts should be awakened and she'll want to join you by licking it. It is crucial, however, to get the puppy out of its bag quickly if the bitch doesn't do this, because it could start breathing inside, inhale fluid and die sooner or later.

Week-old puppies, with their contented mother. However, this whelping box does not have a crush barrier, so younger puppies could easily become trapped behind a careless bitch.

For the same reason there is a problem if, after having contractions for about half an hour, the bitch does not produce a puppy. This is a sign for veterinary assistance. If you had your bitch checked by your vet during pregnancy he or she should have a note as to when whelping is expected, so don't hesitate to ring the surgery if matters are not proceeding as they should.

Puppies fail to appear for various reasons, one of which is a 'breech' birth or presentation. This means that instead of the puppy travelling to the outside world head first, in sensible streamlined pose, it is sliding along the chute tail first. Quite a number do this, some 40% in fact. Most make it without difficulty, but if it is the first, especially with a bitch giving birth for the first time, the puppy's rear end doesn't expand the birth canal as well as its head would, so it may get stuck and require assistance. If you can actually see its legs protruding you can hold them between your fingers and pull gently in time with the bitch's contractions. This should produce a successful result. Otherwise call for professional help. Other reasons for a puppy not appearing are primary and secondary inertia, when either the uterus stops contracting or the bitch becomes exhausted; both require your vet's attention.

The Samoyed

We'll assume all has gone well. You have cleverly removed the wet bedding – newspaper or old blankets under the bitch – which got soaked when the waters broke and messy with the birth. You now have a well-licked, clean and dry puppy nuzzling contentedly at a teat, paddling its forelegs strongly as it feeds. Then, after half an hour or so, your bitch shows the faraway look in her eyes again, strains and pants, goes quiet again, starts again... and so on until the second pup arrives. Another gush of water... another bag... the process is repeated and everything gets wet and stained again - including the first puppy! That's the way nature is and it's going to happen with each birth, so there is a lot of mess. You may decide to change the bedding only a couple of times.

What you may not realise is how cold the puppies can become during the repeated births. Remember they've just come from a highly protected environment with the temperature much higher (about 38.6°C or 101.5°F is the normal rectal temperature). Though one sign of imminent birth is that the bitch's temperature drops a degree or so, it doesn't plunge to that of the outside world. However, the puppies have done just that and now can get really chilled very quickly before their bodies gear up with the food their tummies are taking in for the first time. Maintaining heat at this time is essential therefore, but make sure it is safe and won't burn the pups and their mother.

Then there are the placentas. At some point each one, which surrounds the puppy in the womb and provides its life support system, having done its job, has to be expelled. Ideally the rules would state that after each puppy its placenta would follow, before the next birth, but it isn't always that neat. Placentas arrive somewhat spasmodically. However, the first usually appears reasonably quickly, which is a good thing, because the bitch will eat it – and because it looks awfully messy this activity is best not watched whilst you're having a cup of tea and a cream cake to keep up your strength. Nature cleverly decrees that eating the placenta supplies iron rich supplement for the bitch just when she needs it to stimulate contractions of the womb. It also cleaned up and removed a potential source of infection from the holes her ancestors dug in the wild to have their puppies. Iron rich – so it is dark red in colour. Its arrival messes up everything again, including the puppies already born if they get in the way. They do!

The bitch doesn't have to eat every placenta. Indeed, later on, nature will take its daily course and she will have messy motions that will stain her fur a greenish-black colour, so you can certainly remove the later ones to prevent her having diarrhoea. The stains can be washed away with soap and water.

Although the arrival of the pups should be at about half-hourly intervals most don't read the timetable too well. Sometimes you wait an hour or more then two, possibly three, arrive quite quickly. Looking at our kennel book a typical entry is :

Bitch's second litter: mated 13th day; whelped 60th day. Puppies – dog: 8.40 am; dog (breech): 8.50 am; dog: 9.20 am; bitch: 10.0 am; bitch: 10.20 am; bitch (breech): 11.40 am; dog: 11.50 am; dog: 2.30 pm.

On occasions such as this it is most difficult to tell after the last-but-one puppy whether that is the end. The bitch's previous litter, 19 months previously, comprised six puppies, so seven seemed very pleasing indeed. If your vet has called during the whelping and given an injection to stimulate contractions you are virtually certain that all puppies will be born and there is no danger of one remaining, dying in the womb and causing life-threatening toxic problems. Just to prove us wrong, the eighth and last one in this litter, after a much longer gap than between any of the previous ones, finally made his entrance. Incidentally, only one of these puppies entered the show ring, but he became a champion. Was it this one, we wonder, who knew a thing or two about attracting all the attention? He certainly had ours that day!

That litter meant one of us didn't go to work that morning. Others were more considerate, depending on your viewpoint, and started, for example, at 9.00 pm and finished at 5.30 am. Others, also, were not so numerous; our range extended from one to eight, but Samoyed litters of up to thirteen are known. Occasionally we had litters with one or two stillborn puppies, and there was one in which all but one were stillborn. Then the person who had that puppy later faced the tragedy of its death when it found and ate slug pellets. Dog breeding, like showing, and life in general, has its good and bad moments.

Occasional problems

If you become thoroughly involved with the breed and have litters over a number of years, you'll find that nature is successful in the majority of births but certainly not all. Naturally, you want to have problem-free litters with every pup a winner, but it is unlikely to be so. You will sometimes be faced with a lifeless puppy. If it doesn't respond to the bitch's licking, rub it vigorously as we described earlier and shake it head downwards to get fluid off its chest and out of its nose, especially if you can detect a heartbeat by putting fingertips on each side of its chest. It is worth doing this for some minutes, pausing periodically to see whether you can see the slightest twitch. If you can, keep at it, for this is a positive sign. However, there will be times when an apparently well-formed puppy never responds. The more you rub it the drier it becomes, so it lies in your hands looking a perfect little Samoyed but without the spark of life. You can hardly believe you have to discard it, and doing so is most upsetting.

Occasionally, there will be another one which, perhaps, takes some time to breathe, then does so but seems to have difficulty in feeding. The bitch may even knock this one to the side and ignore its plaintive squeaks, which soon become weaker. All your protective instincts are aroused and you try hard to reverse its downward spiral. However, in the great majority of such cases the puppy will not survive and you'll watch the inevitable law of the survival of the fittest. You may not like the fact, but your loving pet bitch has an instinct in such cases and you will do best to accept her lead.

A worse scenario, fortunately very rare, but nevertheless one which does happen occasionally is when an entire litter is stillborn, or fades and dies. There is no single reason for this. You may find, if you have post mortem examinations, that the litter had a specific defect. One or two have come to our notice recently where all the puppies had cleft palates, meaning that each had a gap in the roof of its mouth and consequently could not suck, so had no future. The kind response was to have them put down. Research reveals that this condition is inherited. You will understand, therefore, our concern that you should enquire about such matters before deciding upon the mating. The anguish of watching a whole litter fade is extremely distressing both to you and your canine partner, the mother.

Other warning signs that things are amiss are a smelly discharge from the bitch's vagina, lethargy on her part, cold puppies although the surrounding air temperature is correct and thin, weedy cries from the puppies rather than deeper, more purposeful sounds in the competitive thrust to feed. Any suggestion of abnormality should be referred immediately to your vet.

The worst eventuality of all is the death of the bitch. Fortunately, that is the rarest occurrence but, again, it does happen sometimes. All we can advise is to ensure your bitch comes from lines without whelping problems, is kept fit and active, is properly fed and is regularly checked by your vet when she has her annual booster injections. That way you will reduce the awful possibility to the absolute minimum.

Hand rearing

Should the worst happen, or the bitch be unable to feed puppies for some other reason (the best would be that she has too many), you may have to hand feed. At first you will probably have to use a premature baby's feeding bottle, but later you can substitute a small baby's bottle. Good equivalents to bitch's milk, such as Lactol or Welpi, can be bought from good pet suppliers and should be given at blood temperature; for Samoyed puppies about 13ml of made-up milk to each 100g of body weight in the first week of life, increasing gradually to about 22ml per 100g body weight in the fourth week.

If you are totally hand rearing from birth you will have to feed them every two hours at first, day and night, which we know is very tiring. Fairly soon, if the puppies are thriving, this can be eased to every four hours day and night. At first very young puppies don't sleep all night; they feed whenever they're hungry and the supply is normally available.

Very young orphan puppies should be kept in an open box on towels with a hot-water-bottle underneath, which needs to be changed regularly to maintain heat. The towels need to be warm, not hot, to the touch of your hand. Feed them one at a time, then turn the puppy on its back and gently massage its genital region with a small piece of cotton wool. This mimics the action of the bitch's tongue makes the puppy urinate and pass motions. At first it cannot do this without stimulation. This is another of nature's arrangements to keep the nest clean, for the bitch licks up everything the puppies produce.

Caesarian section

If your vet has advised a caesarian section for one reason or another, provided that your bitch is fit she will probably come through without further difficulty. However, suddenly finding a crowd of puppies around her as she recovers from the anaesthetic can be surprising to say the least, especially if she has never given birth before. She may be quite opposed to their wish to get at her teats. Not having given birth naturally means she may not be getting the right message from her hormones. You may have to spend some time with her, loving and caressing her but being quite firm that she cannot push the puppies away. If she adores your attention she may co-operate; once the puppies start to suck all should be well. One snag is that a side effect of anaesthetic sometimes causes the bitch to hold on to her milk; it may be some little time before the puppies' sucking makes her relax and she lets it flow.

NORMAL POST-NATAL CARE

Let's now return to the normal scene, the majority of cases when things proceed as they should. As soon as you are sure all the puppies have been born, try to get the bitch to go into the garden to relieve herself. She may even have wanted to do this during the birth if the process was extended. Periodically you should offer her drinks of water, or milk. She'll immediately want to get back to her puppies and check them over and they probably will be yelling madly at her brief departure.

Apart from giving her drinks, keeping her reassured by occasionally talking to her and checking that all is well with the puppies, you should leave her comparatively undisturbed for 24 hours. Her intake of fluid is very important to keep up her supply of milk to the puppies, but she also needs rest. Just be within earshot in case one adventurous character goes on an early exploration spree and gets behind her back and under the crush barrier. It will let you know quite vociferously and she may wonder where all the noise is coming from.

Over the years we've had plenty of friends who, facing their first litter, have telephoned us for assistance. We don't mean just the odd call – we mean about every half hour for the best part of a day and night. We've been glad to respond. We can imagine that, in the future, technology will improve and it will be possible to telewhelp using shared real-time video rather than just talking on the phone and depending on people's powers of description to advise about what's happening. However, as we emphasise on such occasions, we are not vets; nothing replaces professional advice from people who are properly trained. You may decide to contact your friends for help but don't expect them to be omniscient. Experience helps but it cannot replace veterinary knowledge.

CHAPTER nine

Rearing and Selling Puppies

It never ceases to amaze owners how quickly a bitch gets all her puppies looking neat and tidy. Certainly the second day seems totally different from the wet and mess of the first. Hopefully, you can now begin to enjoy the wonderful feeling of happy, contented puppies with a happy, contented mother. All is comparatively quiet and peaceful, apart from the buzzing sound that emanates from the box from time to time as feeding places are changed by nudge and thrust.

Probably you will have weighed each puppy at birth, though if you leave this for a few hours there won't be much difference in each. You should weigh them regularly so that you can check progress for the first fortnight or so. This means you have to know which puppy is which, and that isn't as difficult as you might at first imagine. If there are both dogs and bitches that reduces the problem. Then, say, you have four dogs. At first their pigment is entirely pink so you can't yet see patterns, but the weights will probably be different. Typically there'll be one heavier dog, one lighter one, and two in between. If you compare the heaviest one with the lightest, side by side, you'll soon spot variations; the breadth of the head, size and position of the ears, possibly even the texture of the coat. Once you have spotted some differences, take the other two and compare them, looking for such differences. Here they may be less obvious but there will be some. No two puppies are identical.

After some days pigment begins to darken and this considerably helps identification. Pink pads get some black spots, which gradually become patches, then extend over the entire paw. If you look at the large pad on each left front paw, for example, you will soon find different patterns developing, which you can draw and name. Our puppies have enjoyed such temporary names as, 'the ace of spades'; 'little two spots'; 'big two spots'; 'no spot'; 'three corners', and so on. It's quite enough for you to be sure which is which for the first eight weeks.

After three days we advise you to ask your vet to remove the puppies' dew claws. We are well aware of current thinking about not altering the natural dog and we certainly concur with that in relation to Samoyed breeding and showing, with this single exception. The dew claw has no use but, if an adult dog catches one awkwardly, it can produce a nasty injury. Whether a dog has them should be of no consequence in the show ring.

Care of the bitch

Provided the bitch was well prepared for the birth by being properly fed and exercised she will look after the litter entirely for the first three weeks. The puppies' demands on her resources increase during this period, so you must continue to feed her properly. She may find two meals a day preferable to one large one. She will certainly need plenty of fluid, and we suggest some of this should be cows' milk. Normal vitamin supplements for nursing bitches are advisable and calcium tablets can be given following the first week after the birth. Do not continue giving these after the fourth week because, as is so often the case with useful substances, too much calcium can be dangerous to her health.

'Phew!' A two-week-old puppy takes a breather.

The puppies' eyes open at about 10 days. Gradually, between then and about three weeks, the puppies become more lively and adventurous, scrambling all over their mother, who tolerates this benignly. As soon as they seem likely to climb over the low front of the box, either remove it or put in another section to keep them in place for slightly longer. One point needs watching, or rather points: puppies' nails soon grow. With the paddling motion they make when suckling you may find the area around each teat becoming sore and the bitch may well object. Snip the tips of the nails carefully to remove the sharp points.

By about three weeks there will be occasions when the bitch is quite happy to have a little time away from them. A sensible arrangement is for you to have a puppy play-pen with nice clean bedding, such as Vet Bed, into which you can put them for periods. The bitch can see them if she wants to check up but they can't get at her, so they'll gambol over one another until they're tired. Then they'll crash out, which is very peaceful. The pen may also be a good place for you to start the weaning process by offering the puppies their first 'solid' food in a place where their mother can't eat it. Also feeding them away from her may prevent her following nature by regurgitating her own food to give them some that is partly digested. That is something you'll want to avoid in front of a fastidious neighbour who has come in to see your 'darling puppies'!

Weaning

Scraped raw beef is the best for the very first attempt. It isn't messy and is natural food for them. Put some on a flat surface so that the puppies can walk up to and smell it. They'll experiment with their mouths as they do with everything; soon one or another will have a go at eating it and very soon the rest will copy. Once a day is sufficient at first, and soon you can change from scraped to very finely minced meat. Soon, also, you will be able to add very fine puppy meal.

If you decide to use baby food instead, or proprietary puppy weaning food, your puppies will probably do perfectly well, but the feeding process will be a messier affair. They seem adept at plastering themselves all over before

'It's all gone, dear, but you can try!'

getting much in their mouths. Their mother will enjoy licking them, though. The puppies should also be given the chance to experiment with drinking from a saucer. Use milk at first, which they will see more easily, then let them try water. After they've bathed in it a couple of times they'll be able to focus on it and drink. Once they are used to more solid food you should increase the meals to four or five daily. The diet should be balanced, so either use a prepared puppy food or ensure they have meat, biscuit meal, a milky meal such as rice pudding, and vitamin supplements daily. Include calcium as well, following the manufacturer's guidelines, and it is sensible to do the same with the bitch.

It is a very good idea to feed the puppies together but on individual plates. They are used to competing for food when suckling so if you isolate them may not eat much. When you line them up one to a plate, one or two will wander off and try others, so they'll finish up two or three to a plate. Then they'll look to see what's left on the other plates and polish that off. Make sure there is a reasonable amount for all so that the feeding doesn't become frenetic. You'll find they each eat a reasonable proportion this way; if you do have a greedy one it will finish first, not eat the lot. If it does try to overdo it you can remove it. Keep an eye on them all at first just in case one does lose out entirely, but next time it's hungry it should get the message that it needs to be quicker off the mark.

Get some worming medication from your vet and give this when the puppies are three weeks old and again at five weeks, doing the same with the bitch. Despite the fact that you wormed her before you may find the puppies have them in surprising numbers. Dose them again before they leave for their new homes and give some medication to the new owners. Getting rid of roundworms is easy; letting them develop inside puppies can be disastrous because they take away so much nourishment and can soon damage vital organs.

From about three-and-a-half to four weeks the puppies become boisterous, jumping all over the bitch and enjoying her playing with them. When she's tired or sends them away they'll chase you when they are free, chewing at your shoe laces and buckles, trouser ends, toys, fingers when you tickle them – anything which they can get into their mouths. Ensure that anything and everything is safe, which means too large to be swallowed. They have milk teeth at first but these are remarkably sharp, as you'll know if one decides there's some tasty meat on a finger bone!

If the weather is good you can let the puppies experience the big, wide world of your garden from four weeks onwards. Watch them carefully all the time. This is sensible for reasons both of safety and assessing developing personalities. You will soon spot who is the most adventurous, or whether you have one which is rather timid in strange surroundings. Most are naturally curious and they may well taste plants, twigs, leaves and anything else available, even soil. Do your best to stop them, and certainly ensure they cannot possibly do this with anything poisonous, such as laburnum pods, yew, or nightshade weeds. You may need to check a gardening book.

After a supervised romp you can put them in a puppy-pen. Ensure it is in shade if there is strong sunshine; equally, ensure it is not in a cold and strong wind if the weather is fine but wintry. As with so many other aspects of puppy rearing it is a matter of common sense. Don't imagine that because Samoyeds' natural home was Siberia you can suddenly take your puppies out of a centrally-heated room and leave them outside in cold conditions. If you do you might as well write a cheque for the subsequent treatment at the same time.

Selling

From four to five weeks puppies in a litter are boisterous and adorable. At six and seven weeks they are very boisterous and still adorable. From eight weeks onwards they are exceptionally boisterous and, if you have a sizable litter, there will be times when your adoration will flag a little. By ten weeks matters are serious and desperation may set in. Twelve weeks doesn't bear thinking about.

Ideally they should be moving off to their new homes by about eight weeks of age. There their boisterousness is channelled just as your bitch's was when you had her as a single puppy. To follow this timetable you need to have had an eye to it a long time before.

One dish for each puppy.

If you are breeding because you are involved in the show scene you may have friends who have more enquiries than they breed puppies. If your bitch is related they may pass on one or two to you if they know your bitch is having a litter. The owner of the stud dog may do the same. Probably you will be a member of one or more breed clubs. It is a good idea to let the Secretary know, as general enquiries often come to that person. If you have never shown you may have to advertise. If you do, avoid publications that take advertisements from obvious puppy farms because you won't want to have your good stock tarred with the same brush.

It is our experience that people who truly 'fall in love' with Samoyeds will wait a long time for a puppy recommended by a trusted and experienced breeder. If you haven't joined a breed club we advise you to do so because then you can be known by such people. You don't necessarily have to show; you don't have to attend any meetings or functions, but if you keep in touch with people by phone and letter you will develop very useful contacts for the occasions when your bitch is to have puppies. If you chose her with care, having regard to what we said earlier about wanting to do your bit to keep up or improve the standard of the breed, such people will know that your puppies are worth recommending to enquirers.

We advise you to find out the current range of prices being asked for puppies. Often the highest prices are asked for those that are sold commercially and are not home-bred. Well-known breeders usually ask reasonable prices; reasonable because, although dog showing, breeding and rearing are expensive, Samoyeds are their hobby. They look to recover some costs but with no stretch of the imagination do they make money if all expenses are taken into account. Pitch your prices realistically and do not make wild claims about your puppies.

Paperwork and other items

There are items you will be well advised to give to the new owner and others you must supply.

You must give the new owner a Kennel Club registration certificate for the puppy you are selling, a transfer form, a correctly written pedigree certified with your signature and a receipt for the money paid.

Blank forms are available from firms specialising in stationery for dog breeders. We advise one showing five generations, which will be more helpful to the purchaser than a shorter one for studying breeding lines if he or she follows in your footsteps later on. Do write all names carefully if you are not typing them. We sometimes see pedigrees on which the names of dogs we bred years ago have undergone changes, obviously due to poor handwriting. This may well cause difficulties for future research.

You should give a diet sheet showing what the puppy is eating and when. We suggest you also add when it was wormed and when the litter was given a health check by your vet and his or her name and address. It may also be sensible to have a space for a note declaring the puppy's weight when sold and to put it on scales in the purchaser's presence and write in the figure. These are sensible points supporting the fact that you are selling a thoroughly healthy puppy. We would also advise giving the purchaser some of the puppy's usual food and a couple of worming tablets from your vet.

Registration and names

You must register the litter with The Kennel Club for it to carry any value. An unregistered dog cannot be shown, nor can its progeny be registered. A note of the registration will appear in due course in the quarterly issues of the 'Breeds Supplement' of The Kennel Gazette, one book of which is devoted solely to the Working Group. The registration will be listed under your name and will include the name of the sire, the name of the dam and her date of birth, references to the Supplements in which the sire's and the dam's registrations appeared, and each of the puppies' names. If, later, the new owner transfers the puppy to his or her name, that transfer also will be recorded in the Supplement.

This information not only informs people about recent litters, but also enables pedigrees to be traced. Many people become interested in the ancestry of their breeding lines or, indeed, of the whole breed. For example, there are books containing the pedigrees of all Samoyed champions from the very first, Ch Olaf Oussa, born 1901. To gain the necessary information The Kennel Club registrations for the entire breed had to be researched. The first two volumes were produced for the Samoyed Association by the late W E (Bill) Lloyd; for subsequent ones he was assisted by the late Margaret Probst. Currently four volumes are published, and a fifth is in preparation.

The matter of registrations and names raises the point of an affix or kennel name. Most but not all registered Samoyeds carry someone's affix. This identifies the breeding to anyone in the show scene, so if a Mr Sibersam has a registered affix *Sleighswift* people know a dog named *Sleighswift Racer* was bred by him. Nowadays, the breeders' affix is put in front of the dog's name, though that is a comparatively recent ruling by The Kennel Club; in the past it was a matter of choice. However, Mr Sibersam could own a dog named *Cudleigh Bear of Sleighswift* if it was bred by, for instance, Miss Champwinner, whose affix is *Cudleigh*. This may or may not be out of Sleighswift parents or lines. When he acquired it Mr Sibersam would apply to The Kennel Club for a change of name from *Cudleigh Bear* to *Cudleigh Bear of Sleighswift*.

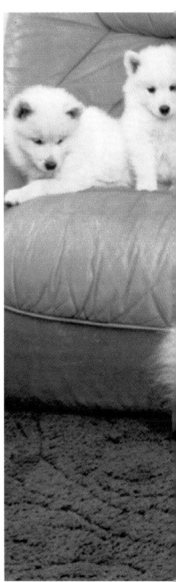

You can register an affix by applying to The Kennel Club on the appropriate form with a short list of the ones you would like, one of which the Club will select, publish and invite any objections. There are limitations on the type of words allowed. Subsequently, your name is granted on payment of an annual fee. Effectively the affix then becomes your trade mark for showing and breeding.

At one time The Kennel Club enforced a regulation that a dog's name could not be longer than 24 letters including the affix(es). People who regularly type records into word processors know that isn't now the case and the names seem to get longer and longer, sometimes with two affixes added because the dog has changed hands between breeders. If you decide to go for a lengthy one, remember you may have to write it many times in the future.

Because we are interested in the history of the breed we suggest that, if you do become thoroughly involved and develop your own breeding lines, you should decide to have a policy of using distinctly different names for all your puppies. Some people choose names with very slight differences, perhaps just one letter, for different puppies or, for example, mother and daughter. On a 10-generation pedigree we have is listed a bitch, Karenina of Kobe, who gave birth to a daughter named Kara Nina of Kobe. You can imagine this leading to research problems when someone is unsure whether two very similar names refer to the same dog.

To identify particular litters by name, breeders often choose a theme name, so the affix and the theme identify both the person and the specific litter. However, it is helpful to future researchers if the puppy names which follow are adequately distinctive, for instance Sleighswift Sirius Wanderer; Sleighswift Sirius Explorer, S S Digger, S S Lover, S S Starlight. Inventing names can be an interesting hobby in itself; as you will see in any catalogue, some involve flights of fancy. Too many Samoyeds have been bred for people to keep to names eminently descriptive of their native ancestry, but we urge you to do your best!

A large, mischievous litter. Their poor mama is out of coat, which is only to be expected.

CHAPTER

ten

The Show Scene

For this section we are assuming that you have never shown a dog before. Perhaps you have bought your first puppy and are wondering how well it might do in the ring in competition with others. Perhaps the breeder has told you it has good show potential; indeed he or she may be encouraging, even urging, you to show. All who breed for the enjoyment of the show scene want to see their best stock in the ring, but keeping many dogs is expensive. Inevitably, good show puppies have to be sold, but hopefully to people willing to try their hand at the exhibiting game.

You will be in good company. The whole show scene is comprised of two groups of people: those who are comparatively new and the long-standing stalwarts. The first group is by far the larger. For many reasons, the great majority do not show for longer than about eight years. If you look at exhibitors' names in a breed in show catalogues ten years apart, probably you will find only a small proportion of people listed in both.

Before we plunge into detailed information about shows and showing, let's consider the broad view of what it is all about. Competition! We human beings are competitive in so many aspects of our lives that we bring it into our hobbies. Indeed competition makes the hobby in many cases, hence flower and vegetable shows, cake-making competitions, Miss Whatever, bodybuilding, drama, choir festivals... and bird, cat and dog shows, to mention just a few. The competition in dogs is not just between exhibits. It is a matter of judging exhibits against a general standard and assessing how well each meets this.

Each breed has a standard, which a judge should know thoroughly as he or she examines each exhibit, handling all parts of the dog and then watching it move in three directions. If, say, there are seven dogs in a class, the mental exercise is to assess how closely each matches The Kennel Club Breed Standard and then to put (probably) five in order according to that match. The best match is put in first place, the next best in second, and so on. This is what a judge should do and this is what you will be expecting when you take your newly-acquired Samoyed into the show ring.

Now judging is not an exact science. It is not like marking a student's page of arithmetical calculations, which are either right or wrong, and adding up the marks to produce a totally objective score. Inevitably there is much subjectivity in judging. The very nature of judging in any sphere involves giving an opinion based on knowledge and experience; for instance our unwritten common law, symptoms of illness, even truth (as parents, teachers and jurors all do). However, you will usually find that a good dog, exhibited at a series of shows over a period of time, is likely to appear more often than not in the placings under various judges. Samoyed show results each year prove the point, particularly so in the case of new puppies, which may win well at quite a number of shows for two or three months. Then, as they start to go through the 'teenage stage', losing their lovely puppy coats, becoming gangling and oddly uncoordinated as they move, they drop out of the placings and sensible exhibitors leave them at home. Later on, if the adult lives up to the potential seen in the puppy, they return and start winning again, though with 'ups and downs' because no dog remains in perfect show condition month after month, year after year.

We have more to say about judging in chapters 11 and 12. As far as exhibiting goes, if you are trying it for the first time, go into it with your eyes open. It is a human activity. The dogs have no conception of what we are doing. Occasionally someone says, 'I'm sure Bonzo knows when he has won because he gets so excited!' Actually, Bonzo would get just as excited if his handler gave him exactly the same fuss and attention and the ringsiders clapped if he was dismissed without a place. Being top dog means something entirely different to a dog and depends on establishing a pecking order in the kennel, for which the services of a judge are not required!

An exemption show at Astutus Pet Hotel.

TYPES OF SHOW

There are six types of show, though you are not likely to find many cases of three of them. The full list is Exemption, Match, Sanction, Limited, Open and Championship. The most popular by far are Open and Championship, with Exemption Shows offering an interesting fun day out, usually in summer. The distinctions are:

Exemption Show

This means *exempt from Kennel Club Show Regulations*, though there are some provisos. The show is open to pedigree and non-pedigree dogs, whether Kennel Club registered or not. It will have some pedigree dog show classes (up to four are allowed) but it can have any number of novelty classes open to any dog. Examples are: fancy dress for both handler and dog; the dog the judge would most like to take home; the most similar pair (dog and handler); best rescued dog... and so on, according to the ingenuity of the organisation arranging the show. Usually the intention of an exemption show is to raise money for a charity or project. Entries are made on the day at the show.

Match

This is a knockout competition at which dogs compete in pairs and the winner goes on to the next round. Sometimes the match is between societies; occasionally handling matches are organised in which the handlers compete rather than the dogs. An interesting form of match was held late in 1996 at the first *Samoyed of the Year* event, at which the year's Challenge Certificate (CC) and Reserve Challenge Certificate (RCC) winners were invited to compete on a match basis.

Sanction Show

This can have up to 25 classes, the highest of which is Post Graduate. It is organised by a breed or a local club and entries are restricted to members and must be made beforehand by a particular closing date. However, you can send a subscription and a joining application form to the club with your entries.

Limited Show

This is very similar to the Sanction, but the classes can be of the full range up to Open, though champions and dogs that have won CCs cannot be entered. Entries are restricted to club members or people living within a defined area.

Open Show

This can be either an all-breed show or a breed club show, and both champions and CC winners are eligible. Some all-breed Open Shows are large events and most breed clubs organise one or more, up to the number they are allowed each year by The Kennel Club.

Sarnoushka Houdini and Novaskaya Zahrek Lafay at the SBOL Open Show, Ampthill, February 1997.

Samoyed Breeders and Owners League (SBOL) Open Show, February 1997.

**Crufts 1997,
at the National Exhibition Centre.**

Championship Show

This is the top level show at which Kennel Club Challenge Certificates can be won. Wins or placings in certain classes qualify a dog to enter Crufts the next year. General Championship Shows are organised by long established societies, some of which have been in existence for well over 100 years and even predate The Kennel Club. Breeds may be allowed one or more championship shows according to the number of dogs registered annually and, if there is more than one club in the breed, The Kennel Club decides which one, or more, will be granted the shows.

THE SHOW CALENDAR

This is no different from the full calendar. There are shows throughout the country throughout the year, if you include all types of show, from those of local clubs and societies to the general championship shows. At the time of writing the major shows for Samoyeds cover 11 months, from February to December. Each of the four breed clubs uses its allocation of championship and open shows and there are plenty of general championship shows where Samoyeds are scheduled. The result, currently, is a spread of 38 shows in 44 weeks. The Kennel Club's allocation of CCs to the breed stayed at 32 sets for a substantial period; after a reduction to 28 it now seems likely to be 30 for the next few years.

CLASSIFICATION AND SHOW ENTRIES

All shows are divided into classes. A schedule, printed well before the show, carries a list of the classes and shows the requirements for entry to each. Schedules are available from the show organisers, which usually means the secretary or the show manager. Announcements about forthcoming shows are published in the advertisement sections of the two weekly dog papers, *Dog World and Our Dogs*, and these will include the name and address of the person from whom schedules can be obtained. Usually clubs and societies send schedules to all people who exhibited at their shows the previous year.

Schedules include entry forms, which must be filled in carefully. The show catalogue, available on the day of the show, carries the details of your entries, including the name of your dog, its parents, your name and address and the classes you have entered. Other people may make use of the catalogue information, for example for keeping breed records. Many exhibitors file all their catalogues and these provide a source of information and interest for many years. Inevitably some errors are occasionally made by people preparing them, so you need to ensure your entries are accurate and carefully printed to minimise the possibility of your details being wrong.

You also have to take care with the closing date for entries, for which the date of *postmark* is normally stipulated. If your envelope doesn't carry the latest allowable date when it arrives your entries are likely to be returned. A snag lies in the fact that some societies are

The SBOL stall, Crufts 1997.

Two veterans at Crufts 1997:
Ch Karazoe Snow Kazam of Samont and Duke of Murmansk.

somewhat lax in this, so exhibitors may be lulled into false security, only to be disappointed when the rules are applied strictly. It's much better to be safe and post a day or two before the final date.

The Kennel Club's *Show Regulations* carries the full list of classes a club or society could use and lays down the provisos for entering a dog in each. In practice, clubs and societies select a proportion and offer these at a show, depending on the expected number of entries. Obviously the organisers hope there will be a reasonable number of dogs in each class. If entries in a breed fall at a particular show the probability is that the organisers will reduce the classification next year, or possibly increase it if the converse happens. Classes may be mixed (for both dogs and bitches) or separate, which is most usual.

The first few classes at a show will be for young stock, with entries restricted by age. The first three listed below are examples of these. The other classes carry restrictions based upon previous wins.

Minor Puppy

For exhibits aged at least 6 months but not over 9 months on the first day of the show.

Puppy

For exhibits aged at least 6 months but not over 12 months on the first day of the show.

Junior

For exhibits aged at least 6 months but not over 18 months on the first day of the show.

Maiden

For dogs that have not won a Challenge Certificate or a first prize at an Open or Championship Show (Puppy, Special Puppy, Minor Puppy and Special Minor Puppy classes excepted, whether restricted or not).

Novice

For dogs that have not won a Challenge Certificate or three or more first prizes at Open or Championship Shows (Puppy, Special Puppy, Minor Puppy and Special Minor Puppy classes excepted, whether restricted or not).

Post Graduate

For dogs that have not won a Challenge Certificate or five or more first prizes at Championship Shows in Post Graduate, Minor Limit, Mid Limit, Limit and Open classes, whether restricted or not.

Limit

For dogs that have not won three Challenge Certificates under three different judges or seven or more first prizes in all at Championship Shows in Limit and Open classes confined to the breed, whether restricted or not, at shows where Challenge Certificates were offered for the breed.

Open

For all dogs of the Breeds and Varieties for which the class is provided eligible for entry at the show.

Veteran

Normally open to any exhibit over the age of 7 years on the first day of the show. Veteran Classes at Crufts carry an upper age limit of 12 years.

Others

At breed club shows there may be other classes, such as Special Beginners. Here the beginner is the owner of the exhibit and it may be for people who have not won a Challenge Certificate in the breed. Other examples are Brace, Team, Stud Dog with Progeny, and Brood Bitch with Progeny. These add interest to a club show because such classes are not seen at the general championship shows throughout the year.

Ch Fairvilla Anastasia winning Veteran at 14: long-lasting qualities and a biscuit coat.

IN THE SHOW RING

When you enter the ring for the first time it's well to be briefed on what happens and why. Exhibiting has the same basic format whatever the level of show. The judge needs to look closely at your exhibit and you need to show it to best advantage. Though this is the same activity the whole world over, in Britain you'll probably not get much more than two minutes for the judge's inspection. This timing is based on the fact that we get large entries at many shows, so The Kennel Club does not allow one person to judge more than 250 exhibits in a day. At a rate of 30 an hour this will take over eight hours non-stop. A typically good entry at a championship show is 150 Samoyeds and this will take at least from 10.00 am to 4.00 pm, with an hour's break for lunch. The overall breed winner cannot be decided until the very end, and then it has to go forward for Group judging, and there may be up to 40 other breeds besides Samoyeds in the Working Group at the show. All this is very time consuming, so you need to make good use of your time.

Exhibitors wear numbers that are often given out in the ring by a steward. He or she checks to see which exhibits are present and records any absentees. Typically, the steward will place exhibits that the judge has not seen in an earlier class on one side, though if the class entry is large this is impossible and exhibitors will occupy the whole ring. In Britain exhibitors can stand where they like unless asked to do otherwise by the steward; in some countries, however, exhibitors must stand in numerical order. The judge may first want to see all exhibits moving round the ring together, that is in a circular line; if the entry is large this may be done in two sections. There is no requirement that this must be done and judges vary as to whether they want it. Its purpose, usually, is to let the dogs stretch their legs, get used to the ring, and liven up. The judge gets a preliminary look at the general standard of the side movement of the exhibits. A quick eye will spot those with good drive and extension (see below).

The judge will then want to see each exhibit individually. Small breeds are judged on a table, but this doesn't apply to Samoyeds, so the judge has to bend down over each dog to feel the major parts of its body and skeleton and assess the quality of its coat.

Now imagine for a moment you are a puppy, in the entirely new surroundings of a ring, with quite a number of other excited Sams around you, and probably with a rather strange feeling coming at you from your 'boss'. If you weren't before, this feeling now makes you a touch apprehensive. Suddenly, someone you've never seen before looms over you and promptly handles you all over, including a quite sensitive place, and even tries to open your mouth and pull your lips back! Of course, being a Samoyed, you're supposed to love all human beings... but, hey, this is going a bit far, isn't it?

Preparation

You must familiarise a new puppy with what will happen well before you take it to its first show. If you don't, what we've just described may put its show career back by many months or maybe wreck it forever. We write with experience. One of our foundation bitches, who appears in the antecedents of many show winners today and who very many people said was undoubtedly of champion standard, simply hated showing. We doubt that we took enough care before her earliest shows. Later, when we knew a thing or two, we took another youngster under a lady judge who not only appeared in a very wide-brimmed black hat but who also decided to test exhibits' fronts by clasping her arms around their chests, lifting them slightly and dropping them. We managed to get that young bitch over the experience, but it took much time and patience.

Judge Barbara Rivers checking teeth at the Windsor Championship Show.

So, before its first show, do get a number of friends to handle your puppy, open its mouth, walk round it while it stands still with you holding the lead. Then lead it away from and back towards your friend, walking it in a triangle. Then change the friend for another, practise on another day... and another... In this way you will help it to accept the experience of being judged in the ring. Most judges will be sympathetic if you mention that it is your exhibit's first show, but the examination should still be thorough. And whilst you are not likely today to get idiosyncratic judges doing something quite unusual, they do vary. Prior practice pays!

Moving your exhibit

When your exhibit has been examined you will be asked to move it. Here, we admit, we write from the judging point of view. To assess movement you need to see whether the dog's legs move backwards and forwards in a straight line extending from the shoulders to the paws when coming towards you, and similarly straight from the hips to the paws when moving away. For this reason, you need the dog to move in a straight line in either direction.

Sideways on you need to see whether the front legs reach well forward and the back legs show a powerful push or drive, whether the front and rear paws on one side of the dog just meet or overlap as they come together, not to mention the topline, or neck, head, ears and tail carriage, and coat appearance. So the judge is most likely to ask you to move your exhibit in a triangle. We hope you can see why from our explanation. We hope you can also understand why it is so exasperating to a judge when the triangle becomes a sort of meandering circle and the exhibitor seems way off line when returning. Or could it be that the exhibitor knows the dog's movement has faults and doesn't want to show them? It does happen, but no judges worth their salt will be taken in. More often than not it is simply sloppiness. Please decide from the start that you will show smartly.

Furthermore, Samoyeds are in the Working Group. This doesn't mean they really ought to be employed here for something like their original herding and occasional haulage work, but it should mean they are active dogs. Indeed, in some countries, they can and do enter activity competitions, and a few in Britain take part in sledge racing. We have already described how, in the United States, they can also gain official titles at various levels in tracking, herding, obedience and other activities. You note the emphasis on action? Therefore, when moving your dog in the show ring, do so with reasonable pace as well as accuracy. In your brief two minutes you cannot shine much as a handler while the judge is checking your dog, but you get your moment when asked to move.

Now that doesn't mean you start demonstrating your acting skills to the ringsiders by moving with exaggerated trotting or prancing yourself. What is required is to show off your dog's good movement, which comes from good breeding and proper exercise, by moving it smartly, precisely and correctly. That, also, needs prior practice. Probably you'll get half a minute – no more. Thirty seconds to show that your dog carries well the centuries of inheritance gained from free roaming herding activity on the tundra and in the forests. Don't heave your dog back and try to make it walk to heel, or plod slowly and uncharacteristically. Move it with pride and panache.

We make no apologies for dwelling on movement. As we write, many people agree that in the show ring Samoyed movement generally is not good. Indeed, we have had letters from overseas correspondents who have seen recent videos of the breed taken at Crufts and other championship shows, wondering why movement has deteriorated. We are sure the reason is the general lack of activity many owners allow their Samoyeds. We have tested this to an extent recently by asking those owners whose dogs do move well in the ring about their exercise programme. Without exception, the good movers get plenty and of the right kind.

Line-up in Open Dog class at the Windsor Championship Show.

PLACES AND PRIZES

When the judge has finished examining the exhibits individually he or she has to decide which are the best and place them in order. Usually these are selected from first down to fifth and placed in the centre of the ring, with the first nearest to the judge's table, as stated in The Kennel Club's instructions. Sometimes, however, if the class is large, the judge will ask a number to come into the middle without placing them, dismiss the remainder and then concentrate on those selected. Perhaps they will be asked to move up and down once again, and then the placings will be made from these.

This is most likely to happen if there is a large entry in a small ring. It is difficult enough to judge an active breed like Samoyeds in a small ring, but if there are, say, 25 dogs packed in, selecting five straight away will not be easy. Nevertheless, the judge would still be expected to complete the whole class, including marking up the results and taking any necessary notes, within about 50 minutes in this case.

At this Danish Samoyed Club Show, model Sammies are painted in the traditional place colours.

Award cards are given, traditionally red for *First,* blue for *Second,* yellow for *Third.* Fourth place receives a card called *Reserve,* usually green and fifth receives *Very Highly Commended* (VHC), usually white. Very occasionally there are more places, for instance in the two breed Open classes at Crufts, where the sixth dog receives a *Highly Commended* card and the seventh a *Commended* card. In the past most shows also awarded prize money for first, second and usually third places. Nowadays this occurs in only a few cases but, understandably, those shows tend to be popular because entry fees have increased considerably as dog showing has become more popular; the prize money is an added attraction.

Shows often have separate classes for dogs and bitches and the classes have varied entry requirements as we explained earlier. Let's suppose there are five classes for each sex. When the judge has finished all the dog classes there will be up to five winners – it's possible for a dog to win more than one class, so there could be less. Typically the steward will call for 'all unbeaten dogs' to come back into the ring so, if your puppy won its class, it will be up to you to be ready to do so. The judge then looks over the winners again, perhaps moving them once, and then selects the Best Dog. Later the same is done with the bitches. The Best Dog and Best Bitch are then judged for Best of Breed (BOB).

Challenge Certificates (CCs)

Really these are a form of prize, but such a special one they deserve a spot on their own. As mentioned above, they are only given at championship shows. A 'set of CCs' given by The Kennel Club at a show may be awarded by the judge as follows: one CC to the Best Dog and one Reserve Challenge Certificate (RCC) to the next best; one CC to the Best Bitch and one RCC to the next best.

The importance of CCs is that they count towards the title of champion. A dog winning three CCs under three different judges, provided at least one was won after the dog became ineligible for puppy classes, can be awarded the title *Champion* by the Kennel Club. The green-bordered certificate presented in the ring is signed by the judge and carries an affirmation that he or she considers the named dog to be *worthy of the title of champion.* A few weeks later The Kennel Club, after checking that everything is correct, sends the real Challenge Certificate to the owner.

The RCC does not carry any special privilege, except that if subsequently The Kennel Club disqualifies the CC winner for any reason, the Reserve is promoted. It is a very rare occurrence, but not unheard of. However, winning an RCC does advertise the fact that a dog is close to championship standard, and a dog that wins two or three advertises the fact that more than one judge thinks the same.

The CC winners are selected from the line-up of class winners in each sex. However, for the Reserve CC the judge may call back the dog or bitch that was second in the class from which the CC winner came. For example, if the Dog CC winner won the Open Class, the second in Open may be invited back to be considered for the RCC against the other class winners if none of them has met and beaten it in another class. This is fair because the

It's a long, thirst-making day! Crufts, 1997.

standard of exhibits varies from class to class as does the number of entries. The Open Class in our example may include a number of champions and the second in the class may well outshine the other class winners. Equally there might be small entries in Open and Limit but a very large number in Post Graduate. If the judge gives the CC to the Post Graduate winner it might be sensible to consider the second for the Reserve CC.

Three more awards are given by The Kennel Club and, therefore, carry status:

Junior Warrant

The regulations for this award were changed as this book was being prepared. To obtain it dogs are now required to gain 25 points based on wins secured between the ages of 6 and 18 months. Each first prize at a championship show is worth 3 points and each first at an open show gains one point. At least 12 points (that is, four firsts) must be gained at Championship shows with CCs on offer for the breed, and at least 12 points (that is, 12 firsts) at open shows or championship shows without CCs on offer for the breed. The owner has to make a claim to The Kennel Club which, after checking the information, sends the Junior Warrant.

This award is not easy to attain because you have to achieve the necessary minimum of 16 first prizes during the leggy and out-of-coat 'teenage' stage through which Samoyeds pass.

Kennel Club Stud Book Number

This replaces a dog or bitch's original registration number when its progeny is registered. To gain an entry and number in the Stud Book the dog has to win a first, second or third prize in a Limit or an Open class at a championship show, or win a CC or a Reserve CC. Details of the pedigree and the qualifying wins are listed in the the Stud Book, which is published annually. Once a dog has gained a Stud Book number it is qualified to enter Crufts at any time. The Kennel Club issues a certificate of entry automatically the first time a dog qualifies for a number.

Groomed, ready and waiting her turn. Crufts, 1997.

Breeder's Diploma

This is issued to the breeder of a Champion on application to The Kennel Club. Thus if the owner is not the breeder the latter can receive due recognition of his or her part in the dog's success.

THE CAMARADERIE

Most people start showing through the encouragement of the breeder of their puppies, especially if you say from the outset that you would like to try. Even if you come to your first show without any other contact in the breed we can confidently tell you that most people who show Samoyeds regularly will be very happy to help if you explain that you are a novice and want advice. In this situation it would be most sensible to visit a show first without your dog, ask for help and watch what happens. Most likely someone will be very happy to take you under their wing for a show or two when you first enter.

The first Samoyed of the Year event, 1996: Averil Cawthera-Purdy with Ch Snowmyth Shamara of Lireva.

If you then come to shows and/or show regularly you will find much friendship. People meet one another up and down the country, in good weather and bad, at indoor shows and outside. However, the point of showing dogs is to take part in competition. This calls for a particular kind of interpersonal skill if you are going to handle successfully both competing and being friends. Not everyone manages to achieve this, and it

Robin Newhouse showing Annecy It's Me at the Samoyed of the Year event 1996.

can be quite a problem at first. On the whole those who find it necessary to be antagonistic in competition usually drop out after a time. It is those who handle it well who gradually become the stalwarts, forging friendships that last over the years, albeit with some ups and downs; the course of true friendship never runs smoothly all the time.

An element of the competition is not only between particular exhibits, but also between kennels. Breeders put a great amount of time, effort and money into developing a kennel, stamped with their affix and hopefully stamped with a recognisable type. Naturally, such breeders are going to feel that their stock is the best. Newcomers may well gravitate to a particular group that shows that kennel's stock almost exclusively.

In the past this was far more noticeable because there were a few very large kennels, such as the three established for the longest periods so far: Kobe, Arctic and Snowland. Their owners differed markedly in personality and background but there is no doubt that, although their rivalry was considerable, each acknowledged those truly outstanding dogs produced by the others from time to time. They also put up outstanding rival stock when they judged.

The key to handling rivalry successfully is to be a sport in the good, old-fashioned meaning of the term. When you lose, which in showing simply means that your dog isn't placed, take it in good heart and congratulate the winner. When you win, don't go over the top. Remember your dog is exactly the same, win or lose. If it is a good example of the breed many people will agree, and this includes judges. A proportion of judges will place your dog. If it really is very good that placing will be first on quite a few occasions. However, no dog wins every time it goes in the ring, so you are bound to have disappointments. So will your friends. We have all been there. So, give or take a pat on the

**The first Samoyed of the Year winner:
Ch Zamoysky Lucky Casanova of Roybridge,
owned by Bridget Enticott, bred by Carol Hamilton.**

back, congratulate or commiserate, go and have a drink with one another (soft if you're driving home!) and look forward to the next show.

At the summer shows a number of exhibitors take trailers and camp, some making a circuit of the midsummer shows, moving from site to site. Some shows are located in lovely parts of the country, amidst beautiful scenery. It can be quite relaxing if, after a full day at the show, you only have to take the dogs for a short walk back to the camper instead of joining the long queue of cars setting off for homes many hours away. Then it's possible to have parties on one another's pads and wile away a gorgeous summer evening telling each other time and again all the judge did wrong, or perhaps right, that day!

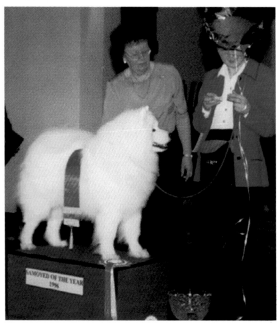

**Northern Samoyed Society President, Joyce Stamp,
with Donna Fleming,
who handled the winner.**

Samoyed line-up at the West of England Ladies Kennel Society (WELKS) Show.

The breed clubs occasionally arrange social events, such as fun days, rallies, and dinners with discos. These are highly enjoyable and give people the opportunity to meet away from the events of the show ring, possibly to make a profit for a charity or rescue schemes. In the past there were Christmas parties for children in the afternoon and a dance for the grown-ups in the evening. Father Christmas appeared with children's presents on a sleigh drawn by Samoyeds lent for the occasion to enable the reindeer to wander off for a while, content in the sure knowledge they could be rounded up easily afterwards!

The events change over the years – the camaraderie does not. We commend it wholeheartedly.

Giving the reindeer a rest.

CHAPTER eleven

From the Centre of the Ring

Occasionally, perhaps, exhibitors driving homeward cardless wholeheartedly disagree with Shylock when he cries, 'O learnéd judge!' He says that when he thinks the judgement about the famous pound of flesh will be in his favour. Later, like cardless exhibitors, he has other views. But you can be sure that ringside comments about judges will never be occasional; they are perpetual and inevitable. The simple fact is that, without a judge, there would be no show.

Judging is the central core, the heartbeat of shows, and in dog showing there is no panel giving a series of individual marks, thus sharing responsibility. Neither is there a pause for consideration, with results or a verdict given at a later time. Every class at every show needs a judge who delivers a decision on the spot... and not too slowly, or exhibitors tend to get impatient! That's how it's been for nearly 140 years and it is highly unlikely that anyone will seriously suggest we change the method.

Because it is so important we want to explain the process: how a judge should assess the conformation and movement of Samoyeds. Then, in the next chapter, we explain how you might begin to judge if you want to do so: how you might progress to championship level; differences you might find if you were invited to judge abroad; and other points of interest along the way. Even if you know you'll never, ever, want to stand in the lonely spot delivering judgements, nevertheless you may find some of our thoughts about assessment useful in understanding what a judge may be thinking in producing a particular line-up. You'll also gain a wider view of the process of showing.

The exercise is to assess dogs in the light of The Kennel Club Breed Standard, reprinted in full in chapter 2 on page 28. That lists the various parts of a Samoyed for which particular points are specified, for instance:

Ears: thick, not too long, slightly rounded at the tips, set well apart and well covered inside with fur. They must be fully erect in adults.

If you had 10 dogs facing you in the ring and had to place them in order according to how well their ears fitted that statement you would probably make a very good attempt. If five people did the same independently using that statement as the guide, probably there would be considerable agreement. Doubtless they wouldn't reach 100% uniformity because there would be some dogs with very similar ears, so the middle order might vary a little.

However, 17 sections in the Standard carry descriptions of elements of the dog, and each has to be considered. The remaining two mention that any departure from the others is regarded as a fault, and that males should be entire. Assessment, therefore, is quite complicated and certainly a stimulating mental exercise. Eleven sections describe specific parts of the body, while the other six are more general: appearance, characteristics, temperament, movement, colour and size.

The judge must handle a dog thoroughly to determine exactly how the body is constructed; this is necessary in a short-coated breed and even more so in the case of a Samoyed with its dense double coat. The judge must also see the dog moving: going away, sideways on and coming towards. However, there is another element not mentioned in the Standard which many exhibitors will argue is also very important: type.

The subject of type in a dog will keep people arguing for ages. It has been discussed since the very first standard was drawn up for the breed and it will continue to occupy us and our descendants in the show ring for as far into the future as we can imagine dog showing continuing. Yet it is extremely difficult to define and there is no doubt that different people have different mental images of a *typical* Samoyed.

In some countries the phrase *judging to type* can be pejorative, conveying the idea that a judge is favouring one kennel. In Great Britain judging to type is usually considered a compliment and means that the judge's placings in a series of classes look similar. Sometimes the opinion may be given somewhat grudgingly, meaning perhaps the speaker's exhibits weren't placed but, 'At least you could see what type he/she was going for!'

So there are three major elements in the task of judging:

- Making an assessment of the dog as a whole and in its parts against the breed standard
- Assessing its movement
- Considering type

We will give some detailed attention to the first two. The third, inevitably, is amorphous – and explaining the idea is rather like trying to create a piece of sculpture with melting ice cream!

Ch Samovar Ice Crystal at six months.

ASSESSING THE WHOLE DOG AND ITS PARTS

The first three sections in the Standard (see chapter 2) are concerned with broad elements: general appearance, characteristics, and temperament. Each carries key points about the breed.

We cannot emphasise too strongly that Samoyeds are medium-sized, well-balanced dogs. All pictures of early dogs in Great Britain and the rather small number of true Samoyeds used on expeditions show this clearly. So does the picture of the one gracing the voting 'booth' in the Jamal peninsular in 1996 (see page 7).

Over the years we have heard all kinds of pseudo-explanations as to why they should be larger. Probably these are really explanations after the event. As a result of good diet and the breeding of larger dogs to larger dogs, size does increase. We discovered that ourselves and found a lovely home with a relative for a dog we bred and started to show when he grew well beyond correct size. In our opinion the fact that people find they have larger dogs should not mean the Standard has to be altered if the intention is to keep the breed as close to the originals as possible. Therefore, if you are judging in the United Kingdom, you should be looking for medium and well-balanced Samoyeds. However, this does not mean small dogs. It is unfortunate that, sometimes, British Samoyeds are called that in comparison with larger ones in some other countries.

At 12 months Sasoolka I Love Trouble demonstrates excellent conformation and expression.

If you are asked to judge in a country where the size provision in that standard is greater than ours you must judge to that. You should not apply the proviso of one country's standard in another, whatever your personal view. If the standards differ, you must know these differences and judge accordingly. We emphasise that the basic requirement is to assess dogs in the light of the particular standard. The Fédération Cynologique Internationale (FCI) and American Kennel Club Breed Standards are reprinted in full in chapter 2 (pages 30 and 32).

Similarly the 'smiling expression' is fundamental to the breed, as is the very affectionate temperament. So you should not place any dog which grumbles at you or is nervous of you – except, perhaps, a puppy at its first show – or place highly one with a heavy, coarse expression and down-turning mouth.

The elements of the Samoyed

Refer to each point in the current Kennel Club Breed Standard for the Samoyed (page 28).

Head and skull: Here it is important that a judge does not confuse *powerful* with *heavy*. The head certainly should be strong and firm, and neither weak nor weedy looking. The wedge is seen when you look down from above. If you hold your hands flat on each side of the cheeks

The points of a Samoyed

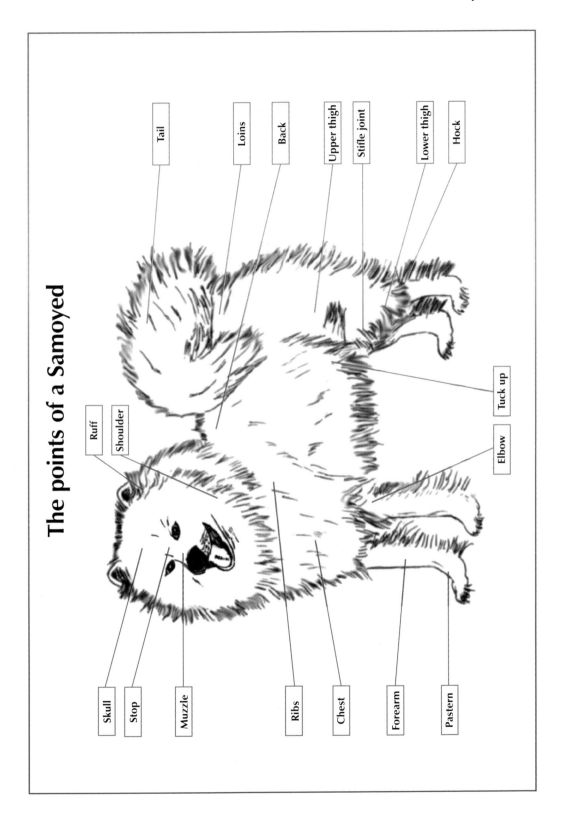

Tail

Loins

Back

Upper thigh

Stifle joint

Lower thigh

Hock

Ruff

Shoulder

Tuck up

Elbow

Skull

Stop

Muzzle

Ribs

Chest

Forearm

Pastern

The skeleton of a Samoyed

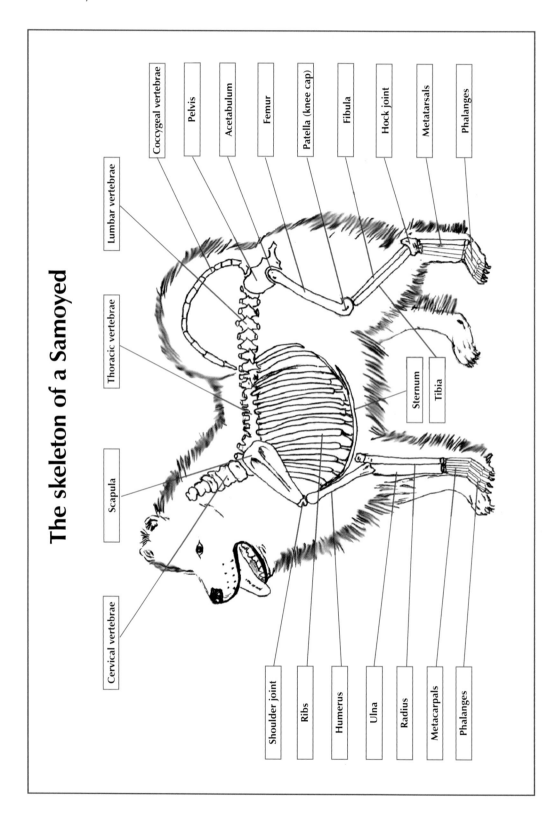

Cervical vertebrae

Scapula

Thoracic vertebrae

Lumbar vertebrae

Coccygeal vertebrae

Pelvis

Acetabulum

Femur

Patella (knee cap)

Fibula

Hock joint

Metatarsals

Phalanges

Sternum

Tibia

Shoulder joint

Ribs

Humerus

Ulna

Radius

Metacarpals

Phalanges

they form the sides of the wedge. *Not too sharply defined* means it should not end in a very pointed nose like a fox; a typical Samoyed nose is reasonably large and rounded and the muzzle curves towards it very, very slightly. Feel the skull between the ears; this should be flat, not domed. The lip pigment should be black; pink sections are considered faults, but a very small pink section should be considered a very small fault. To set off the face, a black nose looks best, but brown or flesh-coloured noses are not faulty.

When judging the head, look for the Samoyed 'smile' – the up-turn of the lips near the ears. You can see this from the side when the dog has its mouth closed, as well as when it is open. Preferably, check it with the mouth closed after you have looked at its back teeth and lips. The eyes must smile as well.

Eyes: Just as in humans, the eyes carry much of the expression in Sams. The really typical ones are slanted and almond-shaped. They should look straight at you when you judge the head from the front, an imaginary line through an eye from inner to outer corner continuing upwards to the outer base of the ear. There should be no gaps in the black pigment of the eyerims. Both light and dead black eyes are faulty; the requirement is for medium to dark brown.

A 12-month-old dog with all the right attributes: Annan Snow Eagle in Johannesburg.

A strong, masculine head, with no trace of coarseness: Hilsar Really Thomas.

A problem for a judge is where to place a dog that is very good in all other respects but has wrong eyes, such as round in shape, and/or too closely set. This is where personal opinion has to operate; how much do you feel the wrong eyes in this case detract from the Standard's requirement for the appearance to be *free from coarseness* and for a *smiling expression?* Having answered the question to your own satisfaction you place the dog accordingly. We suggest it would be well worth a place, but not first.

Ears: Probably these are among the easier parts to judge. The standard is clear, and wrong ears are very obvious in a Samoyed. The one difficulty that some dogs have in store for the judge is that they can swivel them like radar antennae, which is understandable since distant sounds come from any direction in wide open spaces. When this happens the set of the ear is not so easy to spot. What makes it worse is when the dog flattens them as well. In a Sam this doesn't necessarily indicate nervousness. Because it often happens on the move it may be a sensible way of keeping out the harsh wind. Whatever the original reason, some dogs do this more than others. As the judge you have to decide whether the ears are faulty or not, irrespective of this habit. Many judges resort to the sensible trick of throwing a bunch of keys in front of the dog. The ears should snap upright and forward as the dog reacts to the sound and movement. At the same time you can judge the breadth between them.

Mouth: Over centuries Samoyeds were fed reindeer meat and bones, so their teeth evolved only slightly from the primeval state when they hunted. A badly-developed mouth was a disaster for the particular dog, so probably it would never reach breeding age. As a judge you should look for this necessary strength and for the correctness of the bite. Hold the mouth with the lips pulled back and check how the front teeth meet. The requirement is quite clear: *a perfect, regular and complete scissor bite.* Typically a Sam will hold its tongue slightly between its teeth while you try to do this, so you have to develop the knack of pushing it back and getting the teeth together without nipping the tongue.

A lovely bitch's head and expression: Astarki Sulyndi.

You should expect to find the full complement of 42 teeth but this is not specified in The Kennel Club Standard and judges tend not to penalise harshly for a missing one. In some countries this is viewed differently. The FCI Standard specifies the teeth precisely and includes a drawing.

As judge you must consider the state of the teeth. Ideally they should be white or creamy white. Often, unfortunately, there will be staining for one reason or another. In the ring you are not examining them from a vet's point of view but, nevertheless, stained teeth do not look as beautiful as clear ones.

Neck: Judging the neck requires some knowledge of the skeleton (see page 154) to assess its length. You have to bury your hand beneath the ruff, spread your fingers and feel the space between the rear of the skull to the first thoracic vertebra (the start of the back). When you have compared a number of Samoyeds and felt shorter and longer necks, you will know the difference.

The *proud arch* should be obvious from the side view and certainly enhances the appearance of the ruff. It is in no way concealed by the coat. Once you appreciate what a stuffy, short neck looks like on a Sam you will realise how restricting such a feature would be to agile, economic running pace. Indeed the side view of an alert Sam, ready to race away to greet someone, is like the upper part of a neatly-drawn question mark. The neck outline appears virtually a quarter of a circle. Don't miss this if the dog tends to be looking upwards much of the time. You see the arch, or lack of it, when the dog looks forward at something at its own level, when the muzzle is sloping slightly downwards.

Forequarters: To judge the construction of the shoulders you need some knowledge of the skeleton. This will show you the *lay,* which refers to the angle between the scapula and the humerus: the shoulder blade and the upper arm. The straightness of the legs you can check by feeling the bone, looking at the legs as the dog stands facing you and, finally, as it comes towards you on the move.

Assessing *good* bone can be a pitfall – how much is *good?* Our advice is to bear in mind the phrase *overall balance.* If the dog's legs are so thick or thin that your eye is particularly drawn to them when you look at the overall picture there is probably too much or too little bone. Try feeling the legs of such dogs to help you gauge the correct middle range: *good* but not over- or under-done bone.

Body: The back consists of the thoracic and lumbar vertebrae: that is, from the base of the neck to the beginning of the tail. Note the word *medium* again: neither too long nor too short. The reason a reasonably long back is required, and one a broad and very muscular one, lies in the miles of free running Samoyeds

A typical medium dog with correct head and expression:
Ch Whitewisp Sleigh Lad. Photo: Dianna A Lyane

undertook in Siberia. Too short a back curtails speed; too long limits endurance. Medium length facilitates the essential economy of effort.

This also is why the chest has to be deep without being too broad. Free running over hundreds of years put strong hearts and large capacity lungs in the genetic pool. Imagine a chunky, square, barrel-chested Samoyed puffing away trying to catch up with reindeer disappearing into the white yonder and you'll appreciate what you should assess under this section!

Bend down and run the palms of your hands slowly down the sides of the chest. You should feel a gradual curve from a substantial width down to the breast bone at the base. Again it helps your assessment considerably if you can do it with experience gained from having felt slab sided and barrel chests. You will then appreciate the correct midway *spring of rib*.

Hindquarters: The muscles you should check particularly when assessing hind quarters lie inside the back legs at the rear. If these are slack you are looking at a Samoyed who doesn't get much exercise. They should be firm and, if they are, so will be those controlling the back leg assembly.

The stifle angle is that of the tibia and fibula (the lower part of the back leg) compared with the vertical. The reason this should be a substantial angle is to help the leg develop a very firm

Ch Arianrhod Medi Arawn: an excellent example of masculinity with power and beauty.
Photo: Alan V Walker

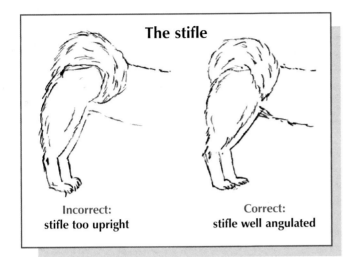

The stifle

Incorrect:
stifle too upright

Correct:
stifle well angulated

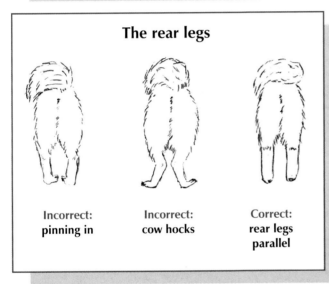

The rear legs

Incorrect:
pinning in

Incorrect:
cow hocks

Correct:
rear legs parallel

push or drive as the dog moves forward. A track athlete gets his or her legs into the optimum position on the starting block; a Samoyed has a built-in starting block if the stifle angulation is good. Conversely, if the stifle is straight, or more upright and therefore at a lesser angle, the push against the ground will be less. With this mental picture in your mind you will easily assess the correctness of stifles.

From the rear the legs must appear straight, both standing and on the move. At first you may be confused with the length of fur on the rear of the legs. If so, you can improve your mental image by looking at videos, especially if they have been taken with a very fast shutter speed and can be shown clearly in slow motion. Another tip is to watch some bad movement in long-legged breeds that don't carry much leg hair. You'll soon be able to transfer the vision of legs moving towards all parts of the compass to anything off-line in a Samoyed.

Cow hocks are so obvious. If you want practice, cows supply this in abundance. A local farmer will probably let you walk behind a herd coming in for milking... and you'll giggle inwardly ever afterwards when you see a cow-hocked dog!

Feet: This statement, like that for ears, is clear and unequivocal. You can hardly confuse bunchy ball feet with the long, flattish feet of a typical Samoyed. Neither can you mix up the small, rounded feet at the end of the perfectly straight front legs of a cat with those extending from the unusually springy pasterns of a Sam. It is those pasterns that make cat feet so wrong. The Sam's feet were developed to cope with the rock hard ground and ice over which the dogs ran for so much of their time. That is why genes decree a long and slightly spread foot.

The soles require plenty of hair between the pads to repel snow. If the hair is not

Ch The King's General of Annecy: a beautiful and very well constructed male.

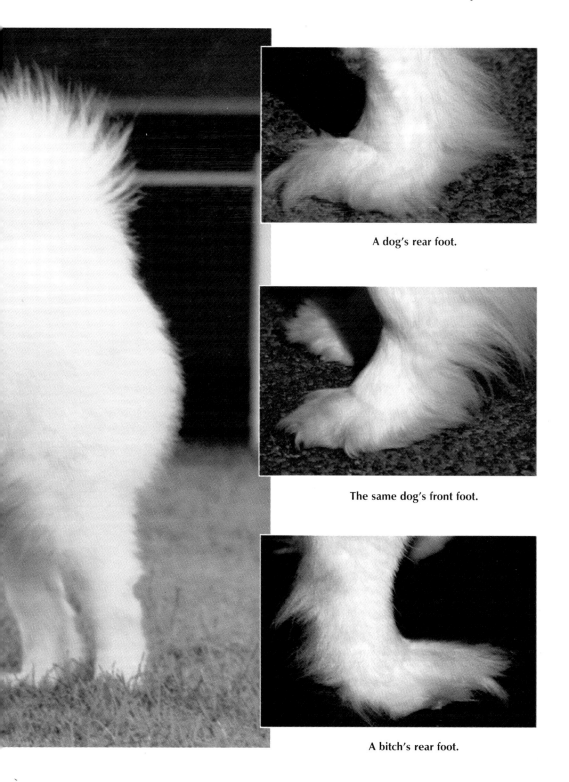

A dog's rear foot.

The same dog's front foot.

A bitch's rear foot.

sufficiently full snow will penetrate, turn to ice, and cause cuts and much discomfort. The fact that it is present ought to explain its genetic origin – if it caused a problem it would have disappeared long ago. Sams who collect balled snow between the toes don't have enough hair there. Remember, the carpet with the closest pile resists water best. Judges should lift a paw and check by putting a finger between the pads. If it goes in very easily the pad is not well-cushioned.

A judge should also be alert to the fact that occasionally an exhibitor trims the hair on top of the dogs' feet. We regard this practice as wrong because it alters the overall appearance of balance. It also prevents the judge from knowing whether the exhibit would carry good feathering. In Great Britain much is made of the fact that Samoyeds are unaltered for reasons of fashion; most people, and certainly the veterinary profession, are very happy with that. We are aware that in the United States this and other trimming is done. When judging there you must accept the fact, just as you do when judging breeds with docked tails and other deliberate alterations. In Great Britain we esteem feathered feet, but the AKC Standard has a different view (see chapter 2). Trimming never has been accepted in the British Samoyed show scene and we hope it never will be. A judge in Great Britain faced with obvious trimming should treat it as absence of feathering and penalise the exhibit in comparison with a well-feathered dog.

Tail: Everyone will certainly agree that the tail is a highly important part of a Samoyed, curving gracefully over the back and falling to one side, with long and profuse strands of hair extending well beyond the tip. It was also highly important for a far more mundane reason: when the dog lay down to sleep in cold and snow it could curl the tail round and cover its nose with the long hair for vital protection. A judge should remember this utilitarian reason and realise that a short, wavy, badly-set tail would be much less effective for one of its functions.

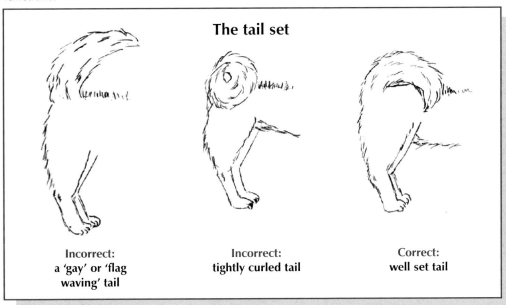

The tail set

| Incorrect: | Incorrect: | Correct: |
| a 'gay' or 'flag waving' tail | tightly curled tail | well set tail |

An example of a well set tail.

Because Sams invariably carry their tails over their backs it might be thought that one that doesn't do so all the time is faulty. The standard allows that the tails may be dropped when *at rest,* but a tail could be carried that way because it *is* faulty. A judge should check the set of the tail (see the Skeleton, page 154) by examining this when looking at the back.

Coat: The coat is of immense importance and was crucial to the dog in Siberia. The most important element has always been quality. A *thick, close, soft and short undercoat* was vital in resisting the vicious wind chill, as well as water whenever it wasn't frozen. The outer coat also played a crucial part as the first line of defence, breaking the drive of the wind and carrying water away and downwards rather than inwards to the skin. In assessing the coat you must feel it for quality and texture as well as for quantity and density. If, when doing so, you remember why heredity has produced what the standard states, you will realise why it should stand straight away from the body and be free from curl. Curly coats would beget curlier coats and water would hug the curls and go inward.

The problem judges and exhibitors face is that Samoyeds shed their fur. Some owners aver their dogs instinctively know when show entries are to be submitted, wait until they are posted, then shed devastatingly! Should they be shown out of coat? Should an attempt be made to keep the coat 'in', even though it is loose and consequently cannot be groomed properly?

Because it is of such importance to the dog as well as contributing much towards its appearance in the show ring, a judge normally will penalise its absence. The extenuating circumstance would be in a young class where most are between puppy and adult coats, or in an adult class where an excellent type dog with everything else of high standard but out of coat is against dogs with coat but also with significant faults. Even then, to put a very-out-of-coat dog first over well-coated ones requires considerable confidence by the judge.

Colour: This is unequivocal. Samoyeds can be white, and many of them are. They can be white and biscuit, and many of them are to some extent, especially as they grow older. They can also be cream, but very few are.

A judge must accept this if he or she is to do the job correctly. A preference for white, for whatever reason, should play no part in assessing the dogs in the ring.

Ch Hemshire Snow Bear, top CC winner 1996 (seven CCs, two RCCs).
Photo: Carol Ann Johnson

Why many coats carry some biscuit is dealt with elsewhere (see chapter 1). It is of genetic importance to the dog in Siberia, but so is the whiteness; hence there is a need for both, with white predominating. Thus the statement in the FCI Standard clarifying white and biscuit colouring is based on correct background: *The basic colour should be white with slight biscuit markings, and must never give the impression of being pale brown.* However, in judging in the United Kingdom judges should note that the Standard carries no such proviso.

Size: The Kennel Club Standard has kept this size level (dogs: 51–56cm or 20–22in, bitches: 46–51cm or 18–20in) since the beginning. There is no reason to alter it if the medium, well-balanced dog is to be retained. A 10cm spread of size is considerable. Most British dogs and bitches are nearer to the top of those limits than the bottom and most judges and exhibitors would consider a 46cm (18in) bitch very small. Antarctic Buck measured 54.6cm (21.5in).

The measurement is to the top of the scapula (shoulder blade) bones on the back. You can feel these quite easily; there will be about a finger-and-a-half gap between them. When judging you should know where 56cm (22in) reaches on your leg. Then, if you want to check height you can put your leg against the dog and spread a finger between the right spot on the back and your leg. Make sure the finger is level.

Larger dogs do appear in the show ring. The point is that size in dogs, as in humans, conforms to the normal curve of distribution, where the majority are in the middle part of the curve. If judges regularly put up a tall dog to the point when he becomes a champion, there is a tendency for people to choose him as a mate for their bitches. Inevitably, he passes on potential for height. If this happens with a number of exhibits the potential increases. Over time we have certainly seen periods when height, generally, was on the increase, while at others it decreased. It really is important for judges to accept that the true skill lies in selecting the typical medium dog – at least in Great Britain and anywhere else where the original size is maintained in the standard.

If you are judging to the FCI Standard be aware that the height range is 54–60cm for dogs and 50–56cm for bitches. In the USA the range is 21–23.5in (52.5–58.75cm) for dogs and 19–21in (47.5–52.5cm) for bitches.

Ch Taronakits Kustom Maid for Nikara in excellent bloom.

Faults: The Kennel Club standard concludes with the statement that *any departure from the foregoing points should be considered a fault and the seriousness with which the fault should be regarded should be in exact proportion to its degree.*

No longer does it list faults, as do others that help judges better. Judges can be sure that

Eng, Am & Can Ch Whitewisp Snow Crystal.

faults listed in other standards would be similarly regarded here. However, what our British standard does say is actually very stringent: *any departure* from all the above is a fault.

Many Sams with faults appear and the judge has to assess the degree of each. The danger then arises that the judge will make comparisons by assessing faults rather than by considering what attributes the dogs do have that match the requirements. We suggest that that leads to an unfortunate attitude: the assumption before a judging appointment that nearly all the dogs you'll see will be pretty awful. Inevitably there are occasions when this is so, and frankly the experience really is depressing, but it is better to develop the positive approach and look first for the good points of each exhibit. Generally these are highlighted in judges' critiques.

Note: The statement that *male animals should have two apparently normal testicles fully descended into the scrotum* comes at the end of every Kennel Club breed standard. So what do you do with a dog with only one descended testicle, or neither?

The word is 'should', not 'must'. Dogs that are not entire can be shown. However, unilateral cryptorchids (one testicle not descended) and cryptorchids (two testicles not descended) tend to pass on these features. Therefore a judge should be wary of giving firsts to such dogs, provided there is good competition. You have to judge according to the circumstances. If you are faced with the situation of there being only one dog in the class and he has this problem, if he is worthy in other respects you might consider withholding first and giving a second prize. This sometimes happens with a puppy class. Incidentally, the term *monorchid* means a dog *has* only one testicle.

Assessing gait or movement

According to The Kennel Club Breed Standard, the ideal *Samoyed moves freely with strong, agile drive, showing power and elegance.* From what we have said already you can see why a Samoyed should move like this... free running across the frozen land with the best possible conservation of effort. Anyone following his or her Sam when it is walking freely on open ground can see it. The movement *is* strong; seemingly they never tire. It *is* free; try to keep up with them and you'll find you have to jog. The gracefulness ensues from the ease of the movement. At the correct speed they seem perfectly harmonised. No strain is apparent in the drive.

It's one thing to see a Samoyed running freely for miles, but quite another to carry that mental image into the confined space of a ring, possibly populated with another dozen or so dogs. The judge must try to interpret the few steps a dog can possibly manage there against what he or she has seen 'in the country'.

When a dog is moving away or coming towards, the judge should be watching to see the legs moving backwards and forwards in a single plane, swinging from the hips and shoulders without a hint of sideways deviation. At the speed possible in the ring the legs should maintain a space between them equal to the width of the body. In free running, as speed increases, the legs come closer in under the body at the paws until the dog virtually 'single tracks' to maintain balance. However, you won't see anything like that in the ring, where the pace cannot be fast enough even if the handler walks briskly – the way to show the gait as correctly as possible.

Sideways the judge should look for extension of the front legs: the forward reach as the dog increases pace, seemingly eating up the ground ahead. At the same time the drive of the rear legs gives the impression that the dog is pushing the ground away behind it. As the legs come together on one side, the paws should not overlap; if they do the dog will have to slew slightly sideways to avoid contact. Thus the size of the leg should be such that, with front leg extension and rear leg drive, the paws almost meet in the middle but don't actually touch.

However, there is more to movement than gait. Viewed from the side, the dog's back should remain level. The judge should

Ch Annecy's Turn Back The Time.

check to see that it doesn't bounce up and down as the dog steps out. Nor should one end rise and the other slope away, betraying to the judge that the front and rear assemblies don't balance one another. For the same reason the judge needs to watch the head and neck carriage to check whether poor construction somewhere is producing an odd result, such as an upright shoulder that makes the head and neck bob up and down on the move.

A correctly moving Samoyed naturally holds its head slightly more forward than at the stance when moving the short distance possible in the ring. When free running it will be held further forward to maintain balance.

Invariably the tail is carried over the back on the move. If it is held down the judge should suspect a faulty set, in which the point where the tail bones begin is not at the end of a level back but after a distinct downwards curve.

With all this to look at and consider while the dog walks in a brief triangle the judge has to develop very quick eyesight and understand what is being demonstrated. It comes with practice which, of course, doesn't have to be limited to judging appointments. Anyone can sit at the ringside; with careful positioning you can see the three sides of the triangle. Try to see at least one section from directly in front or behind, then hope you get some exhibitors who move their dogs straight. You will soon develop the 'seeing eye' for movement.

Although movement in a ring is so restricted, it is very important and a good judge should not place highly a poorly moving Samoyed. To do so is to open the door to other poor movers. That is how the general standard of movement deteriorates. It also encourages exhibitors who hardly allow their dogs any real freedom, carting them from home prison to show bench prison and back again the whole year round. That does nothing for this active breed and judges have it in their power to discourage it.

Considering type

Although it is so difficult to describe, some judges get reputations for *liking a particular type*. This is understandable because each develops a mental picture of what he or she thinks represents the Breed Standard and places dogs that best approach that image. For this reason, dogs in their line-ups tend to be similar.

However, some classes may have only a few exhibits of widely differing type, or one exhibit may have a range of excellent qualities but one item stands out like a sore thumb, such as wrong eye shape, or perhaps size is greater than it should be. What help can be offered the novice judge in such circumstances?

The dilemma is whether to dismiss the dog altogether or have a line-up comprising three similar exhibits with one rather different. There is no simple rule-of-thumb guide to resolve the problem and, probably, experienced judges will differ with very sound reasons for their actions. The most difficult situation comes when a dog is excellent in coat, body construction and movement but has a head which the judge considers unsatisfactory. Should you 'head judge' and dismiss it or consider the old adage *there's a lot of dog behind the head* and include it in your line-up? Maybe you should consider the possible effect on breeding stock in making a decision.

Ch Annecy's A Winter's Tale.
Photo: David L Lindsay.

To give more substantive advice: imagine the very good dog has light eyes. Certainly this detracts from the expression, but perhaps they are the correct shape. The genetic background to light eye colour is such that it can easily be removed from breeding stock because it is recessive. For this reason, an otherwise good dog with light eyes could be placed, even given a first. Indeed, rather light-eyed Samoyeds have became champions, though we hardly commend the fact.

However, a dog who looks excellent but moves badly needs to be thought about very carefully if it is to be placed in a line-up of good movers. Does its poor movement come from lack of muscle tone, which may suggest lack of exercise, or poor construction, which is hidden from ringsiders by an excellent coat but felt by the judge during the examination? Construction faults take longer to breed out. Or could it be that the dog has not been well and is recovering, or has had a heavy litter? Too many implications hang upon this problem

Ch Icemist Beauty of Kobe (left) with Int Ch Gogolev Corbesky.

and the Standard is very definite about movement.

Whether movement is part of type may be arguable. Probably the most obvious elements making up the concept of a typical Samoyed are expression, outline and coat. These can easily be seen from the ringside, which is why they are highly considered in ringside judgements. Together they do form a considerable part of what the judge is assessing, but by no means the whole. The structure can only be assessed by the judge's hands and close scrutiny. That is why, quite properly, the judge makes the decision – alone.

DOGS AND BITCHES

The Standard only differentiates these in the matter of size and weight. However, their bodies and coats differ significantly and a judge should bear this in mind. Typically a bitch has a lithe, slightly finer body, especially in her younger years. The breadth of the back is slightly less than in males, whereas the length should be very slightly greater. Bitches' coats tend to be shorter and more plushy than dogs', with less long hairs in the ruff. This provides the obvious outline of a bitch and is why it is usually easy to tell them apart, even at a distance.

For this reason masculine looking bitches and rather fine, slightly feminine looking dogs are not typical. A judge should not be taken in and place highly a bitch who, for example, has a very attractive head with all the right attributes – for a dog!

AGE CONCERN

No, we don't mean judges should be pensioned off at 65 like test cricket umpires. We want to emphasise that the best Samoyeds are slow maturers. The reason, again, lies in their ancestry. A dog who aged rapidly and was old at eight or nine with the physical limitations of age would be of little use to his nomadic owners in Siberia. No doubt, over time, they selectively bred from the long-lasters because these were more useful and therefore more valuable. Judges should know this and accept that correct Samoyeds do not reach their prime until four or five and then remain in it for many years.

For this reason it is not advisable to select a puppy for a top win, unless the dogs in the higher classes really are disappointing. A very early maturer may look lovely at a particular point in its development, but you fall into a trap if it is eleven months yet looks like a four-year-old and you put it up nevertheless.

Quite often Samoyeds gain CCs and Best of Breeds from the Veteran class, underlining the point. A few have gained Group placings at what, for other dogs, would be very advanced ages; the classic case was Ch Gogolev Corbesky, fourth in the line-up on the day at Crufts at eleven years of age. That it happens less today doesn't mean the breed has altered. Rather, it is because judges assume that any dog must be 'over the hill' beyond about seven years of age.

Samoyeds usually make it to twelve to fifteen years and remain active for much of that time. Then, when they go, they tend to do so quickly. You can understand why, and judges should be aware of this typical life profile.

Int Ch Gogolev Corbesky.

CHAPTER
twelve

Becoming a Judge

After the last chapter you could be forgiven for thinking that judging is so complex and fraught with problems that you couldn't possibly contemplate it. The reality is that only exceptional judges bear in mind everything we have written, and very few of us are in that category. As with everything you have to start somewhere and, hopefully, improve with practice. Furthermore, there can never be such a notion as perfection in judging. How could it possibly be measured?

MAKING A START

If you want to develop new skills in most walks of life you find out where you can be trained. In Great Britain, The Kennel Club is developing a scheme for training judges, though there was none previously. Some breeds, including Samoyeds, have provided help in recent years, but the basic element of a 'trained eye' can be developed to some extent by the individual.

You may well remember that, when you saw a group of Sams for the first time, you wondered how anyone could differentiate between them. Now, no doubt, you can see differences very easily, so your eye has developed to quite an extent. Start taking the process further by comparing many photographs, watching intently from the side of the ring, making comparisons between Sams as they walk about in and out of the ring, and watching your own critically as you take it, or them, for walks.

You can also volunteer to act as a ring steward. Quite often stewards are very busy, so you may not get much time to watch each exhibit being judged in detail, but you are nearer the action. You really start to see exhibits more from the judge's point of view and, given a fairly small ring, from close by.

The point is that, during these quite varied activities, you keep asking yourself varied questions:

- If I had to choose between these two (or three or four) dogs, which would I put first – and why?
- In this photograph, do I think the front part of the Sam is in balance with the rear – if not, why not?
- Which of these three heads is the most attractive to me? Why?
- I'm walking right behind this dog; are its legs moving straight back and forwards from the hips down to the paws?

- Which of these dogs has the best coat? Why?
- This photograph shows a Sam sideways on, over-stretching its back legs. Why? Has it too long a back, is it because the rear end assembly is larger than the front, or from the way the handler is standing has he/she made it stand that way?
- I've watched all exhibits in this class move towards and away from me from where I'm sitting. Which do I think was best? Second? Third? Why?

And so on. Compare and contrast every time you have the opportunity to look at numbers of Samoyeds, in real life or in pictures, wherever they are and whatever they are doing. It is not the same as going over them with your hands, and it is only part of the judging process, but it is very good training for your judging eye.

Then ask some friends to let you go over their dogs. Occasionally, they will be training new youngsters for showing and want precisely this help, so you both benefit. They will want their new exhibit handled a number of times. You then have the chance to feel the various sections of the body on different dogs, go away and check drawings of the skeleton and muscles, and try again with your improved knowledge. It's also easier if you start with dogs with less coat.

The next opportunity you may get is to attend a breed seminar. Typically such events are arranged voluntarily by people in the breed to give opportunities to prospective judges. The programme will probably consist of a general talk on the background to the breed, a detailed explanation of the Breed Standard illustrated with live (and patient!) Sams, possibly a video of movement, a chance for hands-on examination of various dogs, and finally a question session to a panel of experienced breed judges. Such events can be very enlightening and can both improve your knowledge and help you further towards deciding whether you want to try your hand at judging.

Let's assume that you decide to go on. What comes next?

The answer, invariably, lies with a breed club. If you are this far involved with the breed no doubt you will be a member of at least one breed club. Let the secretary know that you are interested in being considered as a judge at a rally. Most clubs organise some kind of kaleidoscopic event, which is partly a fun day, partly a mini-show, partly money-raising for the club or, more often, for a good cause, such as a rescue scheme. The classes provide an excellent chance for a novice judge. It's just like the real thing – ring, exhibits, handlers, placings, prizes and all – but no one takes the results seriously to heart. You get a protected environment in which to make your first judging essay, and others get a chance to see how you do it and what your line-ups look like in the few classes.

In the ring

Perhaps it is useful at this point to explain what you have to do in the ring apart from going over the dogs. In a normal appointment you will have a ring steward. You should read the Kennel Club's Regulations for Judges well before your appointment; in these you will find that you, not the stewards, are in charge of the ring; they are there to carry out your instructions.

We have mentioned elsewhere (chapter 10) that an experienced judge should spend about two minutes per dog, but you also have to record the placings you've made in the judge's book, which you are given when you first report to the organisers at the show. These placings have to be repeated three times on tear-out sections to be sent to various places, including the results board at the side of the ring. Usually the stewards do this chore for you once you have written in the numbers of the exhibits you have placed.

Always the winner, and possibly the second and third, are then asked to remain in the ring while you write notes on them for your report. When you do this for the first time you'll be surprised at how long it can take. Therein lies the pitfall: time! Two minutes for each exhibit should include writing notes and recording placings. If the class has 10 dogs this time scale gives you 20 minutes from the time they walk in to the moment the next class walks in!

The likelihood is that you will take longer than this for the first couple of classes for two reasons. The first is that you will be familiarising yourself with the dogs on the day. Standards vary from show to show and at differing times of the year. The second is that you won't want to hurry the puppies, which need to settle. Owners will appreciate your patience.

You can appreciate the need to establish a routine for each class and to keep to it fairly closely. There isn't much time to chat to the stewards, have a word with each exhibitor, pause for many cups of coffee, then wander off to the loo! Judging is an active mental exercise, bolstered by the need to work to a routine. Once you have experienced the process and are confident you will find you can do it in an apparently relaxed fashion, while understanding why judges do seem to have a 'far-away' look in their eyes!

The notes you make have to be written at speed and also need a routine. Establish some form of 'shorthand' which enables you to cover the main points you want to comment upon, for instance: *ex hd, cor eye, sm ear, gd mth, ex tpl, cor ct, ex tl. 4 st, sw, gd dr.* At home you'll translate that into: *Excellent head, correct eye, small ears, good mouth, excellent topline, correct quality coat, excellent tail, good four-square stance, showed well, good drive on the move.* It's a quick appraisal from head to tail, followed by showing ability and movement. Alternatively, use a small tape recorder.

At a relatively small show with a few Samoyed classes the time scale is not so important. Nevertheless, as an exhibitor you will probably have experienced a slow judge, so you know how frustrating this can be, and how easily you can transmit the frustration to your dog, making matters worse. From the beginning, be determined that you will try to keep reasonably to time. Then, when you are much more experienced and face a very large entry at a show where time is vitally important, you will cope well. You will also delight exhibitors on those frustrating days when Samoyeds are second, or even third, in a ring and the previous judges plod through their classes at a snail's pace. When you judge your classes swiftly and surely and get your Best of Breed into the Group judging by the skin of its teeth, you can allow yourself a warm glow of satisfaction and a suitably large drink when you get home!

After that digression we must get back to your development progress. In the past we would have said that the next stage would be a small show, such as a sanction or a limit show. At the present time, however, these are very rare in the breed. Far more likely is the possibility of your breed club's secretary giving your name to an area club that puts on Samoyed classes at an open show. Organisers of such shows are often on the lookout for breed judges and they know that exhibitors are likely to support classes for a judge who has been recommended from within the breed. If you get an invitation to judge classes at such shows you should accept it gratefully. In this way you will start to build up a number of classes on your judging record. Hopefully, also, you will be improving as you do so.

The next possibility is to be invited by a breed club to judge one of its open shows. Sometimes a club invites two judges, one to do dogs, the other bitches. In this way two people get the experience rather than one, but conversely each gets half the number of classes at the show and therefore less on their record. When you reach this level you'll know why that record is important. To explain it we'll look at judging at the 'top' end.

JUDGING AT THE 'TOP' END

In Great Britain the whole of dogdom is controlled by The Kennel Club and this obviously includes regulating all shows. However, in the matter of judges, The Kennel Club appoints only judges at championship show level. The organisers of all championship shows have to submit names of the judges they propose for each breed at each annual show. Each name is then considered by the Judges' Committee of The Kennel Club and, when passed, is published in *The Kennel Gazette*. Until it is, incidentally, the appointment cannot be advertised by anyone including the person concerned.

So what happens when a person is first invited to judge a championship show and award Kennel Club CCs? The show organisers send their invitation to the new judge and a questionnaire requiring full details of each class he or she has judged, at which shows, when, how many dogs in each class and how many absentees. The prospective judge is also asked how many dogs of the breed he or she has owned, the names of those that have become champions and the names of those with entries in the Kennel Club Stud Book. This information is checked by The Kennel Club. Incorrect information of any kind given on such questionnaires is regarded as very serious, even if unwitting. There have been a few quite spectacular suspensions of well-known judges for this reason.

After checking all details, The Kennel Club sends a request to the breed organisations asking for their opinion on the proposed new championship level judge. If the breed has a Breed Council, and there is one for Samoyeds (see chapter 4, page 57), the request goes to the Breed Liaison Officer. Forms are then sent to the candidate asking for details of his or her experience. Photocopies of this comprehensive information are sent to the clubs, enabling them to consider fully the proposed judge. There are separate forms for breed specialists and all-rounders because slightly different information is needed in each case. When consideration has been given by the members of a club's committee they vote their acceptance or otherwise. These votes are then recorded by the Liaison Officer and sent to The Kennel Club for the final decision by the Judges Sub-Committee.

The Kennel Club requires the Breed Council to maintain an agreed list of judges. This is divided into A1 and A2 lists, both of which are divided into breed specialists and all-rounders. The former contains the names of judges who have already judged at championship show level, and the latter the names of those whom the breed would support to judge at this level but who have not yet done so. The Kennel Club also requires each club to maintain a B list containing the names of people the club would support to judge without CCs. This is sometimes called a club's Open Show List.

The four Samoyed clubs, acting through the Breed Council, decided that the breed's agreed list of judges should be the combined lists of the clubs. This is updated annually and sent to The Kennel Club. The Samoyed Judging List is therefore unusually large.

Qualifications for consideration for approval to be placed on the judging lists of the four Samoyed breed clubs

For qualifications to be considered for approval to award CCs (the A List), 1 and 2 of the following must be met and any one other:

1 To have been on a British Kennel Club registered Samoyed Breed Club Open Show list for at least three years.
2 **For a breed specialist:** to have judged a minimum of 40 classes of Samoyeds over at least a five-year period from the time the person began judging.
   For a non-breed specialist: to have judged a minimum of 50 classes of Samoyeds over a five-year period from the time the person began judging the breed.
3 To have bred or qualified either one British Samoyed champion or two Samoyed CC winners, or bred or qualified five Samoyeds for entry in *The Kennel Club Stud Book*.
4 To have owned Samoyeds for at least 10 years.
5 To have awarded CCs in at least one other breed.

For qualifications to be considered for approval to judge on the Open Show List (the B List) two of the following must be met:

1 To have judged at least 4 classes of Samoyeds with a minimum of 20 at a KENNEL CLUB licensed show.
2 To have owned or regularly handled Samoyeds for at least five years.
3 To have bred or qualified two Samoyeds for entry in *The Kennel Club Stud Book*.
4 To have awarded CCs in another breed.
5 To have made an assessment of Samoyeds at a breed club function – such assessment to have been observed and approved by at least three breed specialists who award CCs in the breed.

Your progress as a breed judge

To return to your development as a new breed judge. At some point, you will reach the level of experience described above for a B List judge. You might then ask that your name be considered, though it is most likely the club officers will know of your interest and be watching your progress. The list will be reviewed annually. Most probably, because clubs need a supply of new judges, if you have been seen to be making reasonably good decisions with the exhibits you have had, the club will want to put you on its B list.

The move from a club's B list to the A2 list will take some years. At least three are needed according to present agreed requirements, though it will probably take longer because of the need to gain much more experience and build up a more extensive log of classes judged. Sensibly, for a breed specialist there is also the expectation that you will be much involved in showing and breeding.

A breed club decides when to move a person to its A2 list. Because it receives the combined list annually, The Kennel Club can check how long you have been on the A2 list.

Finally there comes the moment when you are accepted to give CCs and you step into the ring as judge at your first championship show. When that happens we hope you will thoroughly enjoy the experience, while remembering that you now have more power to influence breed development by your decisions, because you will contribute significantly to the development of champions. Owners will tend to breed their stock to your choices; people in ages yet to come will write about and trace the ancestry of their stock to your CC winners, especially if they gain their titles. Also you may occasionally have the thrill of giving the first CC to a really promising two- to three-year-old. If people realise you have good judging skills other judges will follow your lead and you can be especially pleased when it gains its title.

Judging at Crufts

The pinnacle is reached when you are invited to judge the breed at Crufts. This is likely to be a once-in-a-lifetime event, so if it comes your way make the most of it and hope that your Best of Breed will catch the eye of the Working Group judge and appear in the Group line-up on television, perhaps even win it and compete for Best in Show. The dampener we have to put on aspirations here is to point out that the agreed judging list for Samoyeds is large compared to most breeds, so by no means all specialist judges have this opportunity.

WRITING REPORTS

In Great Britain there is no official requirement to write a report on the dogs you have judged. However, by long established practice, reports are written for the two dog papers, *Dog World* and *Our Dogs*, both of which always send requests to a judge to do so. The judge is asked to write a comment on each class winner and the names of the second and third for open shows, and first and second for championship shows.

Some guidance is given from time to time as to what these comments might contain and an approximate maximum number of words. They also ask for reports to be sent as soon as possible after the show has taken place because they are news. Reports can, of course, be sent by fax. Sometimes facilities exist for judges to write reports and fax them before they leave the show venue.

Exhibitors expect to read reports. This method of feedback from judge to exhibitor is a time-honoured one, so it is natural for exhibitors to feel disappointed if no report appears. A judge who fails to write a report will not face any official action but exhibitors may well decide increasingly that he or she is not worth showing under. Thus the discipline of declining entries may come into play.

Because reporting is unofficial, there is no direction as to what should be written. Typically comments are very brief and survey the good points of the dog. There is understandable reluctance to dwell on the not-so-good points. Emphasising these may discourage the exhibitor from showing under the judge again. In any case, if the dog has been placed first in a class with a reasonable number of entries there shouldn't be many faults to write about in the winner. However, if there are some general faults the judge may make a preliminary comment on the fact at the beginning of the report, such as: *I was disappointed at the rather poor movement evident in a number of exhibits. In some cases this was undoubtedly due to construction faults but, for the majority, slack muscles suggest it stems from lack of exercise.* On the whole, however, we tend to accentuate the positive in Great Britain. Whether we are right to do so is a matter for discussion.

JUDGING ABROAD

British judges are often invited to judge abroad and that is certainly true in the case of Samoyed breed specialists. Perhaps, in former times, this was because we had better stock than most, but time – and the breed – have changed. Nevertheless, invitations to judge abroad have certainly increased. The reason, probably, lies in the number of exhibits we get at our shows, for there is no doubt that our entries are much larger than in most countries. Most of our championship shows attract entries of 100–200 dogs; a few exceed that. Our judges, therefore, gain extensive experience.

It is delightful to be invited. Clubs offer you great hospitality and exhibitors are very interested to have your views. Shows, and judging, differ somewhat according to the country, and organisation follows the national characteristics. This can mean very thorough and tight organisation in which, as a guest, you will want to keep up to the mark. Conversely, it can mean a more laid-back approach, and you wonder how anything will get going. It does, of course. Often the prizes on offer are quite valuable and, if you enquire politely, you'll find the entry fees appropriately spectacular.

Smaller entries at shows give rise to different perspectives of the role of judge. In some countries, notably in Europe, you will find the judge's report is an official requirement. Moreover, a report has to be written on each exhibit in each class. Official forms are provided, usually in triplicate on appropriate paper blocks. One copy is given to the exhibitor at the show, one copy is retained by the club organising the show, and the third copy is sent to the country's kennel club.

Your first invitation may make you wish you had paid much more attention in language lessons at school. We can tell you that judges are required to write reports in their own language, however you manage to communicate with exhibitors in the ring. The club supplies interpreters who write or type from dictation in the judge's native language. Each form then has to be signed by the judge. Before they leave the show exhibitors collect these reports and usually ask the interpreter for explanations of what has been written. You can imagine that this method of reporting carries certain implications.

The usual scenario is that the interpreters are local students who are trying to improve their

Beryl Grounds judging at an international show at Valladolid, Spain.

English, or whatever is the judge's native language. They may not be 'doggy' people. Two problems emerge in the matter of idiom: the figures of speech with which we pepper our conversational diet (you get the message?) and the phrases we use in describing parts of the dog. Consider, for instance: *This dog has a good lay of shoulder and an excellent tuck-up. On the move I would like a trifle more reach in front. He shows with sparkle.* Care to try rendering that in French, Spanish, Italian, Danish, Swedish? If not, imagine the problem back at home when, armed with an average dictionary, an exhibitor with a smattering of English looks up *lay, tuck-up, trifle,* and *sparkle,* not to mention why the judge should be *on the move!* It is so

**Skardu's Gitana, on the left, winning Samoyed Bitch
at the 12th Exposicion Internacional Canina, Valladolid, Spain, 1995.**

Winning Dog and Bitch at a Samojedhunde Klubben i Danmark (Danish Samoyed Club) show. The ribbons on their leads denote class wins.

easy for us to trip these off the tongue (!) and totally confuse the issue. You will need to think about what you are saying and keep the words, phrases and sentences simple: *This dog has the correct angle between the shoulder blade and the upper arm. The line from the breast bone to the loin curves well. When he walks his forelegs should reach forward slightly more. He is lively when showing.*

Though this is longer it is devoid of idiom. It is simpler and easier to translate and so more likely to inform the exhibitor correctly, which is what your report should do. Furthermore your interpreter has to wrestle with unfamiliar words if you use idiomatic speech. We have seen *trifle* typed as *traighfull* in Denmark. Imagine trying to find that in a dictionary!

Another implication of personal reports for each exhibitor is that these are kept. Should you be invited a second time you may well find yourself judging the same dog and writing another report. You will certainly be embarrassed if the exhibitor places both your reports side by side and finds that in one you reported the dog has the correct tail set but in the other you said this was rather low – the tail does not migrate!

Classes abroad

There may also be differences in the classification in other countries as well as in the method of selecting winners and placements. Some do as we do, but in others you may be asked to give a grading to each exhibit, such as *excellent, very good, good*, and so on. These gradings are recorded on the report form and in some countries also in the breeder's show record book: a kind of log book for each dog that the judge is also asked to sign.

Care has to be taken to find out what the prevailing view is as to what these words mean. Probably *excellent* is just that. *Very good,* however, may well be regarded as *average,* or something like *second best* to us. *Good,* quite probably, really means *poor* and is taken very seriously. In one or two places, giving the lowest grading means the dog can never be shown again. Another confusion arises in that occasionally the gradings are called *firsts, seconds, thirds,* and so on. This means it is possible for all exhibits in a class to be *firsts,* though only one can finish in first place.

Sometimes ribbons are given for these gradings, coloured like our place cards, and exhibitors tie these on the show leads in the ring. As the show proceeds some dogs amass quite a collection.

Having judged and graded each exhibit in a class, the judge then calls back all those he or she wishes to see again for placing. Usually this means the excellents, or firsts, (though if you haven't given enough of these you may ask for specific ones of the next grade). You then place these as we would do from a reduced section of a large class. Obviously, you select the winner and next places from the top grade. If you have to place five in each class it helps if you have given that grade to at least that number.

Usually, you then have a number of classes with a winner in each and judge for Best Dog and Best Bitch as we do. However, if the show is of championship level the Open class will not contain any champions. There will be a special class for these and it is the only class they can enter. You judge that class exactly as the others, but then you have to consider the Best Dog and Best Bitch against the winners of the Champions class, deciding whether your non-champion Best Dog is better than the one you know *is* a champion. This is not unusual

**Again, ribbons are tied to the leads of winners
at a Danish Samoyed Club show.**

because champions tend not to be shown as frequently as they are in the United Kingdom, so the champion class may not have many entries. You then judge the two Best of Sex for Best of Breed.

In championship shows held under FCI regulations the Best of Sex is awarded a CAC, which is the equivalent of a CC. This counts towards the title of national champion in the particular country. If the show is at international championship level the judge can award a CACIB if the dog is of sufficient merit. This counts towards the title of international champion and certainly is not given automatically to a CAC winner. There is no equivalent award in Great Britain; we cannot hold international shows because of quarantine restrictions.

ALL ROUNDERS AND SPECIALISTS

By now it should be obvious that specialist judges confine themselves to one or just a few breeds. If you enlarge your interest in judging and learn about many other breeds gradually you will become an all-rounder. From what we have described you can see that to do this in a number of breeds, a large proportion of the Working Group, for example, will take considerable time and effort. It follows that many all-rounders judge more or less full time.

Kaissa's Beaujolais (11 months) and Danish Ch Nino, out of the same sire, winning at a club show.

Argument as to whether specialists and all-rounders judge Samoyeds similarly are long-standing and will continue. It is inevitable that all-rounders do not have the same experience of showing and breeding Samoyeds over the years as do breed specialists. Were this to be an absolute requirement to judge a breed the all-rounder would be a figment of imagination, for no person could have that level of experience in a large number of breeds. Some people aver that all-rounders judging Samoyeds tend to favour dogs who stand alert and still in statuesque pose, as favoured in breeds such as gundogs, whereas the Breed Standard describes Samoyeds as *full of action, displaying marked affection.* Specialists, they say, know what a Samoyed should be and expect one to be lively and full of animation at all times. On the other hand, there is no doubt that, when the Best Samoyed goes into the Working Group ring, it and its handler will have to wait a considerable time. This is the largest group and the judge may well have 40 dogs to see. In such circumstances it is no good if the Sam gets impatient, bored, or flags.

It is quite proper for a judge, specialist or all-rounder, to consider the 'big ring' when making the final selection for Best of Breed. You want to feel that your chosen best exhibit is not only a good representative of the breed but also has sparkling show qualities. That, in a Samoyed, is a matter of lively rapport with its handler, looking about occasionally at the

surrounding events and generally appearing to relish its active participation amid the other dogs and people.

Samoyed breed clubs invite a mixture of specialists and all-rounders to judge their championship shows over a period of years, and this seems to be a sensible policy because it ensures that some all-rounders experience close contact with the clubs, the exhibitors and the dogs. We hope that this practice will continue, and that the same will

Beryl Grounds with her winning dog and bitch, Kuuran Vallesmanni (BOB) and Tuulian Taina Tarmokas, at Kerava, Finland.

be true of all large championship shows offering Samoyed classes. We exhort all who judge our breed, irrespective of background, to develop and maintain as clear a vision as possible of the proper requirements of the Breed Standard, so that Samoyeds can continue to manifest the grace, beauty and appealing nature intended by their 'western' developers a century ago.

Italian/Int Ch Karazoe Snow Legend, judged BOB by Geoff Grounds in Riccione, Italy (in the wet weather tent!).

APPENDIX

Code of Ethics

This code has been agreed by the four Breed Clubs as acceptable guidelines to all who wish to own or breed Samoyeds.

Breed Standard: All breeding stock should follow closely the official Kennel Club Standard in all aspects with particular attention being paid to temperament of the dogs to meet the first characteristic of displaying affection towards all mankind. Dogs which manifestly depart from the Breed Standard are not suitable for breeding.

Breeding purposes: All breeding should include the objective of improving the overall standard of Samoyeds. Equal weight should be given to type, temperament, health and soundness. Nervous or aggressive dogs are not satisfactory as pets or breeding stock.

Registration: All dogs used for breeding should be registered with The Kennel Club and full details of their pedigrees should be known.

Planning of litters: No one should breed a litter unless he or she has the right facilities for dam and litter and the time to devote proper care and attention to rearing the puppies and the wellbeing of the dam. There should be some demand for puppies before bitches are mated.

Breeding age: Bitches should not be mated before 15–18 months of age and not before the second season, and no later than the fifth year for the first time.

Welfare of the bitch: No bitch should be mated at every season. Bitches should not have litters on consecutive seasons. No bitch should have more than three or four litters and a bitch should not be bred from beyond her eighth birthday.

Stud dogs: Only entire dogs should be used at stud and not before 12 months of age. Members who own stud dogs should be aware of the need to improve the breed and enhance the reputation of the sires. They should refuse stud services to inferior specimens of the breed and to owners who have neither the time nor the facilities to rear litters.

Puppy sales: Prospective buyers of puppies should be screened for suitability and ability to provide long term homes. They should be advised of the characteristics and problems of the breed. These include the need for grooming, exercise and family contact.

Puppy information: No puppy should leave the breeder before seven weeks of age. Each purchaser of a Samoyed puppy should be provided at the time of sale with an accurate pedigree and a Kennel Club transfer form and registration certificate. He or she should also receive a diet sheet and information about training, worming, and inoculation. Advice should be given about suitable books and membership of a breed club.

Puppy variations: No puppy which has any physical defect or shows a clear departure from the Standard should be sold without the buyer being made fully aware of the defect or departure from the Standard. Breeders should replace any puppy which develops a defect to such a degree that on the advice of two independent veterinary surgeons the puppy has to be put down, or they should refund the purchase price. The breeder is to be properly notified before any such action is taken. It is advisable for breeders to take out insurance cover on any puppy they breed for the first six weeks in its new home.

Unwelcome sales: No Samoyeds should knowingly be sold to laboratories, pet shops or dealers in dogs, or to persons known to sell puppies to any of the above. Owners of stud dogs should not provide stud services for such persons. No puppy should be sold or offered as a prize in any raffle or competition. No puppies should be sold to countries where they are not protected by anti-cruelty laws and where there are known social and ownership problems with dogs.

After sales: It should be impressed on buyers that they should contact the breeder in the event of problems with the puppies. Breeders should make every effort to assist in these circumstances. Breeders should be prepared to make adequate arrangements for re-housing if it becomes necessary. They should co-operate with the breed rescue organisations to the best of their ability.

Hereditary defects: Breeders should not knowingly breed from any stock which has heredi-tary diseases. It is advised that all breeding stock be X-rayed for hip dysplasia by a qualified veterinary surgeon. It is advised that all X-ray plates should be submitted to the BVA for hip scoring even if the hips are poor so that a true picture of HD in the breed can be assessed.

Advertising: Advertisements for stock should always be honest, factual and without exagger-ation or distortion.

Conduct: Officers and committees of the four breed clubs are always ready to help with members' problems wherever possible. Members should conduct themselves at all times to reflect credit on the ownership of dogs. Members should not allow their dogs to roam and cause a nuisance to other people. They should accept responsibility for cleaning up after their dogs in public places.

Whelping Chart

Served Jan	01	02	03	04	05	06	07	08	09	10	11	12
Due to whelp Mar/Apr	05	06	07	08	09	10	11	12	13	14	15	16

Served Feb	01	02	03	04	05	06	07	08	09	10	11	12
Due to whelp Apr/May	05	06	07	08	09	10	11	12	13	14	15	16

Served Mar	01	02	03	04	05	06	07	08	09	10	11	12
Due to whelp May/Jun	03	04	05	06	07	08	09	10	11	12	13	14

Served Apr	01	02	03	04	05	06	07	08	09	10	11	12
Due to whelp Jun/Jul	03	04	05	06	07	08	09	10	11	12	13	14

Served May	01	02	03	04	05	06	07	08	09	10	11	12
Due to whelp Jul/Aug	03	04	05	06	07	08	09	10	11	12	13	14

Served Jun	01	02	03	04	05	06	07	08	09	10	11	12
Due to whelp Aug/Sep	03	04	05	06	07	08	09	10	11	12	13	14

Served Jul	01	02	03	04	05	06	07	08	09	10	11	12
Due to whelp Sep/Oct	02	03	04	05	06	07	08	09	10	11	12	13

Served Aug	01	02	03	04	05	06	07	08	09	10	11	12
Due to whelp Oct/Nov	03	04	05	06	07	08	09	10	11	12	13	14

Served Sep	01	02	03	04	05	06	07	08	09	10	11	12
Due to whelp Nov/Dec	03	04	05	06	07	08	09	10	11	12	13	14

Served Oct	01	02	03	04	05	06	07	08	09	10	11	12
Due to whelp Dec/Jan	03	04	05	06	07	08	09	10	11	12	13	14

Served Nov	01	02	03	04	05	06	07	08	09	10	11	12
Due to whelp Jan/Feb	03	04	05	06	07	08	09	10	11	12	13	14

Served Dec	01	02	03	04	05	06	07	08	09	10	11	12
Due to whelp Feb/Mar	02	03	04	05	06	07	08	09	10	11	12	13

| 13 | 14 | 15 | 16 | 17 | 18 | 19 | 20 | 21 | 22 | 23 | 24 | 25 | 26 | 27 | 28 | 29 | 30 | 31 |
| 17 | 18 | 19 | 20 | 21 | 22 | 23 | 24 | 25 | 26 | 27 | 28 | 29 | 30 | 31 | 01 | 02 | 03 | 04 |

| 13 | 14 | 15 | 16 | 17 | 18 | 19 | 20 | 21 | 22 | 23 | 24 | 25 | 26 | 27 | 28 | (29) | | |
| 17 | 18 | 19 | 20 | 21 | 22 | 23 | 24 | 25 | 26 | 27 | 28 | 29 | 30 | 01 | 02 | (03) | | |

| 13 | 14 | 15 | 16 | 17 | 18 | 19 | 20 | 21 | 22 | 23 | 24 | 25 | 26 | 27 | 28 | 29 | 30 | 31 |
| 15 | 16 | 17 | 18 | 19 | 20 | 21 | 22 | 23 | 24 | 25 | 26 | 27 | 28 | 29 | 30 | 31 | 01 | 02 |

| 13 | 14 | 15 | 16 | 17 | 18 | 19 | 20 | 21 | 22 | 23 | 24 | 25 | 26 | 27 | 28 | 29 | 30 | |
| 15 | 16 | 17 | 18 | 19 | 20 | 21 | 22 | 23 | 24 | 25 | 26 | 27 | 28 | 29 | 30 | 01 | 02 | |

| 13 | 14 | 15 | 16 | 17 | 18 | 19 | 20 | 21 | 22 | 23 | 24 | 25 | 26 | 27 | 28 | 29 | 30 | 31 |
| 15 | 16 | 17 | 18 | 19 | 20 | 21 | 22 | 23 | 24 | 25 | 26 | 27 | 28 | 29 | 30 | 31 | 01 | 02 |

| 13 | 14 | 15 | 16 | 17 | 18 | 19 | 20 | 21 | 22 | 23 | 24 | 25 | 26 | 27 | 28 | 29 | 30 | |
| 15 | 16 | 17 | 18 | 19 | 20 | 21 | 22 | 23 | 24 | 25 | 26 | 27 | 28 | 29 | 30 | 31 | 01 | |

| 13 | 14 | 15 | 16 | 17 | 18 | 19 | 20 | 21 | 22 | 23 | 24 | 25 | 26 | 27 | 28 | 29 | 30 | 31 |
| 14 | 15 | 16 | 17 | 18 | 19 | 20 | 21 | 22 | 23 | 24 | 25 | 26 | 27 | 28 | 29 | 30 | 01 | 02 |

| 13 | 14 | 15 | 16 | 17 | 18 | 19 | 20 | 21 | 22 | 23 | 24 | 25 | 26 | 27 | 28 | 29 | 30 | 31 |
| 15 | 16 | 17 | 18 | 19 | 20 | 21 | 22 | 23 | 24 | 25 | 26 | 27 | 28 | 29 | 30 | 31 | 01 | 02 |

| 13 | 14 | 15 | 16 | 17 | 18 | 19 | 20 | 21 | 22 | 23 | 24 | 25 | 26 | 27 | 28 | 29 | 30 | |
| 15 | 16 | 17 | 18 | 19 | 20 | 21 | 22 | 23 | 24 | 25 | 26 | 27 | 28 | 29 | 30 | 01 | 02 | |

| 13 | 14 | 15 | 16 | 17 | 18 | 19 | 20 | 21 | 22 | 23 | 24 | 25 | 26 | 27 | 28 | 29 | 30 | 31 |
| 15 | 16 | 17 | 18 | 19 | 20 | 21 | 22 | 23 | 24 | 25 | 26 | 27 | 28 | 29 | 30 | 31 | 01 | 02 |

| 13 | 14 | 15 | 16 | 17 | 18 | 19 | 20 | 21 | 22 | 23 | 24 | 25 | 26 | 27 | 28 | 29 | 30 | |
| 15 | 16 | 17 | 18 | 19 | 20 | 21 | 22 | 23 | 24 | 25 | 26 | 27 | 28 | 29 | 30 | 31 | 01 | |

| 13 | 14 | 15 | 16 | 17 | 18 | 19 | 20 | 21 | 22 | 23 | 24 | 25 | 26 | 27 | 28 | 29 | 30 | 31 |
| 14 | 15 | 16 | 17 | 18 | 19 | 20 | 21 | 22 | 23 | 24 | 25 | 26 | 27 | 28 | 01 | 02 | 03 | 04 |

THE bibliography

Borchgrevink, C *First on the Antarctic Continent* 1901

Brownlie, Dr Serena *An Introduction to Dog Care* Quintet, 1988

Compton, Herbert *The 20th Century Dog* 1904

Daglish, Eric Fitch *The Dog Owners' Guide* Dent, 1933

Elliott, Rachel Page *The New Dogsteps* 2nd ed Howell (New York), 1983

Evans, J M and White, Kay *The Doglopaedia* Henston, 1985

Goodrich, Juliet T *Pedigree Books of American Samoyeds* Fund Trustees, 1975

Grayson, Peggy *Good Judgement* Kingdom Books, 1997

Jackson, F G *One Thousand Days in the Arctic* Harper & Bros, 1899

Johns, Rowland, ed *Our Friends the Samoyed and the Keeshond* Methuen, 1936

Keyte-Perry, Marion *The Samoyed* Marion Keyte-Perry, 1962

Leighton, Robert *The New Book of the Dog, Vol IV* Cassell & Co.

Llewellyn, G *Homeopathic Remedies for Dogs* Kingdom Books, 1998

Lloyd, W E, ed *Samoyed Pedigrees* Vol I–IV The Samoyed Association, 1963 et seq

Marples, Theo *Show Dogs* 2nd ed, 1919

Nansen, F *Farthest North* Constable, 1898

Puxley, W Lavallin *Samoyeds* Williams & Norgate Ltd, 1934

Samoyed Association, The *The Samoyed*
    2nd ed (1951) and 3rd ed (1961) edited by W L B Bowen
    4th ed (1971) and 5th ed (1995) edited by Geoff Grounds

Shackleton, Sir Ernest *The Heart of the Antarctic* Heineman, 1909

Smoot, Jill H, ed 'At Your Service' *Samoyed Club of America Bulletin*, Vol 22(2) April 1996 and 22(5) December 1996

Wilson, Pearl M and Auckram, Valerie E P *The Samoyed (New Zealand)* 2nd ed: 1975

THE index